Ten and Twenty-Two

A Journey through the Paths of Wisdom

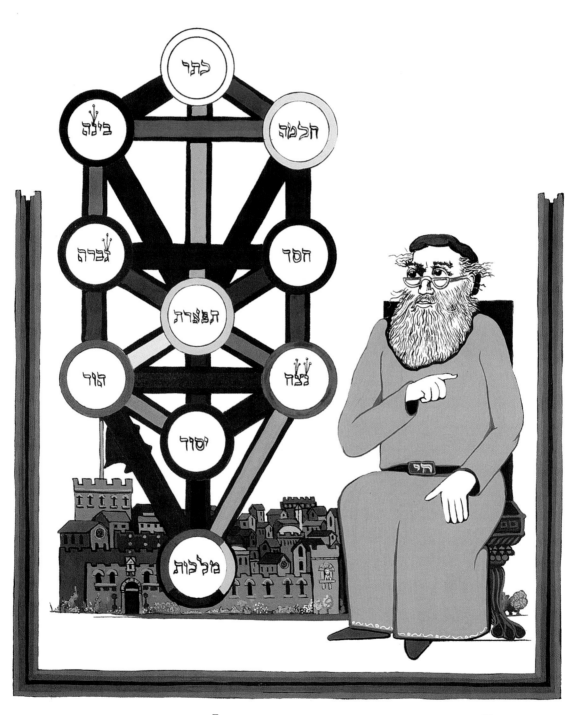

Rabbi William Kramer and the Tree of Life

Ten and Twenty-two

A Journey through the Paths of Wisdom

Michael Jacobs

The Major Arcana of the Tarot,
perceived through the way of
The Tree of Life

JASON ARONSON INC.

Northvale, New Jersey
Jerusalem

Library of Congress Cataloging-in-Publication Data

Jacobs, Michael, 1936–
    Ten and twenty-two : a journey through the paths of wisdom /
Michael Jacobs.
     p. cm.
   ISBN 1-56821-988-1
   1. Cabala. 2. Magic. I. Title.
  BF1611.J33   1997
135'.47–dc21   97-12626

Manufactured in the United States of America. Jason Aronson Inc. offers books and cassettes. For information and catalog write to Jason Aronson Inc., 230 Livingston Street, Northvale, New Jersey 07647.

For my Grandparents of Blessed Memory
R. Haim ibn Yaacov and Leah bat Shimon

לזכר נשמת הורי הורים
ה"ר חיים אבן יעקוב ולאה בת שמעון

CONTENTS

Figures

Acknowledgments

Many people live in my memories, my art, and of course between the covers of this book. I am deeply grateful to each and every one of them.

One sunny summer afternoon in 1994, my friend Arthur Kurzweil and I were taking a break between sessions at the CAJE conference taking place on the university campus of Bloomington, Indiana.
"We'll do it," he said.
"Which part of this conversation am I missing out on?" I asked.
"A book about Kabbalah and Sufism and Tarot and everything else and lots of paintings," was the reply.
"OK," I said.

And so this work was born, with neither of us having much idea of what was involved. We are wiser now.

Were it not for the unflagging support from my wife, Eve B. Greenfield, we would undoubtedly be laboring well into the next century. Her organizational and editorial skills were responsible for bringing this project to an orderly and relatively speedy conclusion. I shall be forever in debt to her depth of perception and ability to bring my somewhat scattered thoughts into focus.

In many ways my Grandparents gave me everything. From them I learned of love and values, of search and exploration and what it means 'to do'. From my Grandfather I acquired a love of books, travel, study and strong Turkish coffee. My Grandmother taught me the meaning of quality, grace and of elegance.

I would like to thank the drill sergeant who taught me the wisdom of reading the instructions on the can.

To Suleiman Loras, of blessed memory, Sheikh of the Mevlevi order of dervishes in Konya, Turkey, I am indebted for the gifts of patience, perseverance and persistence.

No effort of this type would have been completed without the assistance of many people. Foremost among them are Joy Rippel and Kim Ahn whose help both in and around the studio kept all of us moving in the right direction. Our dear friends Judith and Joseph Girard, Leonard and Kelley Anderson were and are a consistent source of valuable support. For a sense of belonging, community, warmth and inspiration I thank the congregation of Ohr HaTorah in Los Angeles and Rabbi Mordecai Finley.

I would also like to thank my students whose enthusiasm for this work was matched only by their willingness to let me get on with it.

M.J.
Venice, California

Foreword

There is a world of mystic, honest mystery, not black magic. In that world are many inhabitants that bear names, beautiful and exotic, transporting and transcendent.

A roll call finds an ideational response to names such as Tarot, Kabbalah, Sufi, Zen, the Order of the Rosy Cross and the like. And once the "like" are called, marshaled in there are the unlike; there being truth in opposites.

In this world the speculative mind conjures up a thousand images from a myriad of sources. If it were not for their "likeness" the images would be terribly different. Near East, Far East, primitive, scientific, naive and sophisticated; they arise from old souls and those yet to be born, causal truth emerges.

There are words without letters. There are shapes without patterns. There are feelings without containment. There is no shortage of abundance in the formless.

The contemplative life does take shape however; in the mind, the visions and the dreams of the speculator. And should that individual be an artist, and should that artist seek to make the invisible visible and the formless have form, order emerges and beauty celebrates it.

Only someone who has dreamt in many languages, had visions in various places and dared not to achieve a synthesis, but to become one, can watch the colors move around and direct them to their places.

Only a scribe bent on telling a story never told before, and yet scribed out of familiar elements, known to the pursuers of the esoteric and the *god-wrestlers*, would dare—and daring achieve—a body of work which is beyond body, to write a lyric which sings with a thousand tongues; which can resonate in ears beyond counting, becoming a melody from the totality of scale into the clarity of a cymbal clashing.

That song is sung by our artist. The work here is the score. And each new visual-listener is transformed to the mountains of Sinai, of Fuji and the Himalayas or even the Mount of Temptations.

NOW EXPERIENCE

William M. Kramer
Professor Emeritus of Art and Religion
California State University

Introduction

As the twentieth century comes to a close, our perceptions and understandings have revealed an exotic, even bizarre world around us. The search for theories which seek to explain all processes has led us on a circuitous and torturous path, which has, in the end, returned us to many of the basic ideas first formulated long ago by numerous unsung seekers on the twin paths of mysticism and orthodox religion.

Today, science admits (albeit unwillingly) that its laws and theories concerning natural phenomena are simply creations of the mind. Understanding this rather obvious fact, we are better prepared to participate in the relationships which exist between the observer and the observed.

Any comprehensive model of reality as we perceive it must contain elements from many disciplines, especially those whose roots stretch back to antiquity. In such a model, the Intangible must be allowed to occasionally give way to the Tangible; and of course the Tangible will, from time to time, be confounded by the Intangible.

M.J.
Venice, California

Part One

The Work of the Chariot

מעשה המרכבה

Kabbalah communicates with human understanding through the language of symbols. The meaning and nature of these symbols is often vague; distorted and changed by the historical process. Problems imposed by transition and translation from one culture and language to another are further enlarged when we are faced with the difficulties of trying to understand the intent of someone born into an earlier culture. Such changes have recurred throughout the long history of the Kabbalah, with each time and culture attempting to use it to serve the needs defined by that society's world view.

In order to illustrate this point we observe that during the Persian, Greek and Roman periods cosmology was mostly concerned with the measurement of the various gods' strengths rather than separating their individual areas of responsibility. To the ancient thinkers, Zeus as exemplified by the Sun, ultimately prevails over Mars simply because of sheer size and correspondingly greater weight. This principle minus the pantheons of ungodly gods was integrated into the Kabbalah and provides the basis for the Attributes of Angels assigned to the Sephirot and the Paths of the Tree of Life. Thus we might say that for these early sages there was no exact meaning for a particular symbol, only a measure of its strength in one or another of the areas of human endeavor. Today, much of the information which was regarded essential in ancient times is rendered obsolete by our western cultures' non-recognition of a multiplicity of gods.

Kabbalah does not describe reality in the way that our senses perceive it, neither does it deal with the materials from which reality is made. Like physics, Kabbalah deals with the laws governing the 'actions' of reality; that is to say that the symbols, alone or in concert, describe behavioral characteristics in relation to the *environment* rather than the *person* as an individual. We also point out that in classical Kabbalah the descriptive process is not limited to the human condition, but to any event, process or thing, which starts in a given place at a specific time.

The symbolism of the Kabbalah when used as a paradigm for life is also seen to change its meaning in parallel with the evolving identity of the individual. Because of this the ancient sages were able to define an individual's behavior in various situations and the nature of his or her reactions to different stimuli.

Thus, in Kabbalistic teachings, the individual's relationship with the environment is paramount.

Emotional, intellectual and physical modeling is performed in and by these symbols, each of which represents a particular dimension or characteristic of the pattern as a whole. Although these characteristics have some parallels in modern psychology it is still necessary to use terms culled from other disciplines in order to present an acceptable model.

The Kabbalah describes several kinds of interaction between the symbols. Each becomes charged with different kinds of information depending on which other symbols are being activated by a particular kind of connectivity.

There are three kinds of symbolic interactions:

Aspirations   Symbolized by the forces governing the sun and the moon.

Actions   Symbolized by the forces governing the planets.

Interactions   Symbolized by reference points in the planetary aspectual circles.

Aspirations are defined by the Kabbalah as being the primary building blocks of behavior which give direction and motivation. They animate human behavior in much the same way that a table might aspire to remain on the floor; not because of some pre-willed decision, but by nature.

Actions and Interactions are characteristics of the evolution and movement of the defined behavior at particular points in space and in time.

The meditations and visualizations we present are rooted in techniques formulated in the early centuries of the Common Era. Although the historical evolution of The Way of the Chariot מעשה מרכבה (maaseh merkaba) is not the subject of this work, a brief overview of the development of the techniques involved seems appropriate.

The Prophets and Psalmists of the Bible, together with the ordinary practitioner of religion, seek to 'know God' and experience the reality of the Supreme Being. Each shares a wealth of visions and revelations of hidden things in descriptions of the mystical experience. Judaic, Islamic and Christian devotional literature are all particularly rich with examples.

The study of mystical experience was traditionally confined to small esoteric groups whose religious background hopefully protected them from heresy. The practices of the initiates of such groups were rarely documented and were transmitted from mouth to ear מפה לאזן (mipeh l'auzen). In the study of early Kabbalistic literature the *Sepher Yetzirah* ספר יצירה appears to contain the most ancient of our source material. This famous work exists today in several versions, the shortest of which contains about twelve hundred words and the longest about twenty-five hundred. Saadiya Gaon (882-942 C.E.) comments that 'the ancients say that Abraham wrote it'. Most of the early commentators of the Talmud and the Zohar support this view. The Talmud lends further credence when teaching that 'Abraham had a great astrology in his heart, and all the kings of the east and west arose early at his door' (Bava Batra 16b). This placement of the earliest revelation of the *Sepher Yetzirah* in the eighteenth century, before the common era, is interesting because it is coincident with the composition of the *Vedic* scriptures in Asia, the codification of *Laws* by Hammurabi, king of Babylon, and the compilation of the *Book of the Dead* in Egypt.

In the Talmud (Berakhot 55a), we find that 'Bezalel knew how to permute the letters of the Alphabet with which the Heavens and the Earth were formed'. Because of this it is said that he was chosen to build the Tabernacle in the Desert. This implies a knowledge of the *Yetzirah* at the time of the Exodus. Bet HaMidrash 6:37 contains the first textual reference to the *Sepher Yetzirah*. Jeremiah, together with his son Ben-Sira, explored the mysteries. There are numerous traditions surrounding them and a certain Yosef ben Uziel who, it is said, was also a Master of the Mysteries. He may have been responsible for a commentary on the *Sepher Yetzirah* and possibly for an early codification of the oral tradition. This placement in time corresponds with the Great Assembly הכנסת הגדולה (knesset hagdolah) and the closing of the Biblical Canon during the period of the Second Temple.

The sages of the Great Assembly codified the ancient traditions into three classifications: Preservation of the Scriptures, Liturgy, and the Oral Law. The chain of transmission extended from the last of the Prophets in the sixth century B.C.E. in an unbroken line, for almost four hundred years, down to the High Priest Simeon HaTzaddik.

4

During the reign of Herod the Great in the first century B.C.E., Menachem the Essene was a vice-president of the Jerusalem Sanhedrin under Hillel. After his resignation at the end of the first decade of the common era he, gathered together a select group of students. One of these, R. Yochanan ben Zakkai was a leading exponent of Merkaba meditations learned from his Babylonian colleagues, prior to his apprenticeship to Menachem. When the Jerusalem Academy was being dismantled, the R. Zakkai was responsible for negotiating the compromise with the Roman authorities which allowed the re-establishment of the Academy at Yavneh in the year 70 C.E. Another of Menachem's pupils, R. Nehunia ben HaKana founded the school which eventually produced the book *Bahir* בהיר, a vital key to understanding the more esoteric teachings of the Kabbalah.

The R. Elazar ben Arakh studied for many years with each of these two Masters and subsequently wrote the *Sepher Tagin*. This important work expounds on the teachings regarding the crown-like flourishes, tagin תגין (Aramaic: crown) used to adorn certain letters in Masoretic texts.   R. Yehoshua ben Chananya, himself the principal disciple of R. Zakkai in Merkaba mysticism, received these special teachings regarding the mysteries of the Aleph-Bet from R. Elazar.

R. Akiva ben Joseph (ca. 45-135 C.E.), was a pupil of both R. Yehoshua and the R. Elazar. With the insights achieved by these studies R. Akiva was able to lay the foundations for exposition of the Oral Law as it was later codified in the Mishnah.

The principal disciple of R. Akiva was R. Shimeon bar Yochai. He was the leader of a group of second century sages whose discussions, reflections and meditations resulted in the first redactions of what was to become the most important work of mystical teaching to date: *The Sepher Zohar* - ספר זהר ~ *The Book of Splendor*.

In his commentary on this period, the early historian Josephus states that the Essenes and the schools which derived from them were able to foretell the future by means of ancient purification and preparations. Prior to this he says, such methods were known only to the Prophets.

The year 220 C.E. saw the final revision of the huge collection of traditions under the title *Mishnah*, by R. Judah HaNasi, usually referred to as 'The Rebbe'. The Talmud states that he taught the mysteries of the Kabbalah to his principal disciples: R. Hanina, R. Hoshia and R. Abba Arikha, also known as Rav, who taught them to R. Yehuda (220-299 C.E.), who, together with R. Aina, founded the academy at Pumpadita which emphasized the use of Hebrew in day to day conversation and prayers rather than the Aramaic vernacular. Among the most influential followers of the methods and teachings of this academy were R. Abbaye Rava (299-353 C.E.) and R. Zeira.

These early Rabbis of the Tannaitic period tended to separate the Mystical Traditions into two separate spheres. The first, called *Maaseh Bereshit* מעשה בראשית (Works of Creation) was not to be taught in public, but transmitted only directly from master to student. The basis for this school was the mystical exposition of the Act of Creation in the first book of Genesis.

The second is the *Maaseh Merkaba* מעשה מרכבה (Work of the Chariot), also known as *Derekh HaMerkaba* דרך המרכבה (Way of the Chariot), and simply as *HaDerekh* הדרך (The Way). Although the restrictions placed on the transmission of The Way were even greater than those placed on that of the *Maaseh Bereshit*; much of its wisdom is still to be found embedded in works such as the Talmud, Zohar, Midrash, and the literature of the *Greater* and *Lesser Heikhalot*. The exponents of both methods were often called *Yordei Merkaba* יורדי מרכבה (Descenders of the Chariot). Their ecstatic visions, methods and results have survived into contemporary liturgy as many of the hymns sung at the High Holidays and the *Kedusha* prayers.

During this long period of codification, the term *Kabbalah* קבלה (Hebrew: that which has been received) was used to identify all Traditions, Laws and Doctrines not contained in the Five Books of Moses. Over the ensuing centuries the term *Mekubalim* מקבלים (those who have received), came to be applied to all followers of the mystic Way. The tumultuous events of the twelfth and thirteenth centuries brought to Europe an influx of mystical and other traditions from Turkey, Palestine, North Africa, Babylon, Central Asia and beyond. The blossoming new schools of thought in Italy, Spain and Southern France distinguished between *Kabbalah Iyunnit*, קבלה עיוני (speculative Kabbalah)ת and the *Kabbalah Maassit* קבלה מעשית (practical Kabbalah). For the most part, *Kabbalah Iyunnit* reached a peak in its development in Palestine. In Central Asia, Arabia and North Africa, the *Kabbalah Maassit* flourished and was greatly influenced by the Sufi and Dervish Masters of the period.

When we pause to compare the religious and mystical writing of authors such as Solomon ibn Gavirol (1021-1058 C.E.), with those of Farid Al~Din Attar (1119-1220 C.E.) or the unknown poet who composed the Cloud of Unknowing, we can only be astounded by their similarity of content.

R. Judah ben Samuel Ha Hasid (d.1217) and R. Eliazar of Worms (d. 1238) were among the founders of the movement known as The Pious of Germany and Western Europe (*Hasidei Ashkenaz*). This school emphasized the special value of devotion in prayer and produced many speculative texts which expounded the mysteries of creation and of the nature of Angels.

In Provence, France, R. Avraham ben David (1120-1198), known as the Ravad, and his son R. Isaac the Blind were important teachers. Their disciples were the first to use the term Kabbalah in the context of purely esoteric teachings *received* as revelation. One of these, R. Asher ben David (nephew of Isaac the Blind) taught the mysteries of the Kabbalah to R. Azriel and R. Ezra of Gerona who were pioneers in the transmission of The Way to the Spanish schools. Under the influence of their teachings R. Moses ben Nachman (1194-1270) known as the Ramban or Nachmanides, became the spiritual leader of the Spanish Jews. His voluminous commentaries are masterpieces of mediation between the metaphor of rabbinical, kabbalistic, and philosophic thought of the time. Outside of the main thrust of Spanish kabbalistic thought was Abraham ben Samuel (late thirteenth century). Known as Abulafia he founded a school of *Prophetic Kabbalah* קבלה הנבואי (*Kabbalah nevoui*) which taught that the true path to the highest stage of contemplation, ecstasy, can be achieved through meditation on various configurations of the letters of the Hebrew alphabet. Because of this, the method is also known as the Path of the Names דרך השמות (*derekh hashemot*).

The formulations of these individual schools continued to mingle and, by the time of the Expulsion of the Jews from Spain and Portugal at the end of the fifteenth century the basic literature of the Kabbalah and the structure known as the Tree of Life had evolved into the form which we know today. The *Ten Sephirot* of the Tree of Life are a manifestation of the Divine Influence as it is channeled through the Four Elements, (Fire, Water, Air, and Earth), and the Four Worlds, (Archetypes, Creation, Formation, and Action). These ten Sephirot constitute the first ten Paths נתיבות (*netivot*) of the Tree of Life and are related to the Minor Arcana of the Tarot (see appendix two). The Sephirot are connected to each other by a sequence of twenty -two Paths which correspond to the letters of the Hebrew alphabet and are associated with the Major Arcana of the Tarot. Thus, the total number of Paths within the Tree of Life is thirty-two.

The visible world is said to be one aspect of a much larger and mostly unseen universe. The work of the Kabbalist consisted of becoming aware of the connectivity between the material and the spiritual worlds. Having reached this level of awareness and aided by the visualizations given by the master of the Hidden Wisdom; each Kabbalist sought to promote harmony between the Upper and Lower worlds. This was achieved through a life of **Right Action** and **Right Prayer**.

During the sixteenth century, Sfad in Palestine became the most important of the new Sephardic centers of the Turkish empire and many great Masters of Wisdom lived and taught there into the seventeenth century. The Messianic flavor of the teachings of Isaac Luria (the Ari) 1534-1572, led to the disastrous failure of the Messianic claim of Shabbetai Tzvi in 1666.

The founder of modern Hasidism was R. Israel ben Eliezer (ca. 1700-1760), the Baal Shem Tov. He brought to a confused European Jewry a simple approach to piety. Although his teachings and those of his disciples drew heavily on the doctrine of Lurianic Kabbalah, they were sufficiently different to be considered a separate path from mainstream Kabbalah; similar to that of Abulafia and his followers some four hundred years earlier.

The industrial revolution of the nineteenth century saw the growth of a better educated, wealthy, and often idle middle class. Together with it developed an interest in a wide range of subjects loosely defined as the 'classics'. Delving into the archives of such venerable institutions as The British Museum in London and the Bibliotheque Nationale in Paris, amateur researchers unearthed numerous Medieval and Renaissance manuscripts. Often in Latin, Greek, Hebrew and Arabic and almost always abstruse in their nature, such manuscripts dealt in the main with the science of the day; astrology and alchemy, mathematics and philosophy, theology, ethics and so on. The Gothic tastes of this era were reflected in numerous lurid and hopelessly romanticized compilations of Grimoires. In 1801 *The Magus*, by Francis Barrett, was published in Cambridge, England. This work spotlighted Islamic alchemy, medieval kabbalistic doctrines and astrology. Successive authors continued in this vein, encouraged by the inordinately large collections of early manuscripts amassed by generations of gentleman explorer-collectors,which were gathering dust in various European institutions. Alphonse Louis Constant (Eliphas Levi), Frederick Hockley,and Montague Summers were among the early explorers and exploiters of the mysteries of what became known as High Magic. During the course of the succeeding fifty years numerous secret and not so secret societies evolved. The Order of the Rose Cross, The Order of the Golden Dawn and the Order of Oriental Templars were typical examples. Kabbalah as understood and popularized by these and other groups, including many orders of Freemasons had a much different purpose than that imagined by the early Kabbalists. With practice, the initiates were able to supplement their own deficient qualities by drawing on those of the universe as a whole. This being the exclusive domain of the European gentry.

The masters of wisdom of both Sufism and the Kabbalah, appalled by the onslaught of such barbarous social Darwinism, retreated in short order to remote areas of Central Asia, North Africa, and elsewhere. These special individuals have remained incognito ever since. Because of their unique diplomatic and ambassadorial abilities the services of these masters were much sought after by the players of the Great Game. Britain, Imperial Russia, France, and Germany.

In the early years of the twentieth century, R. Avraham Kook (1865-1935), chief Rabbi of Palestine from 1921, wrote a series of mystical meditations based on Merkaba visualization techniques. These were published under the collective title 'Orot' (Lights). In 1922, together with R. Zonnenfeld, he approved the founding of the Yeshivat Bet Ulpana LeRabbaniim in Jerusalem. The first director of this institute, R. Yehuda Ashlag (1886-1955) completed the first translation of the Zohar from Aramaic to Hebrew. He was succeeded by R. Yehuda Brandwein (1904-1969), who claimed descent from the Maggid of Mezritch, successor to the Baal Shem Tov. R. Brandwein was the first Jewish settler within the walls of the Old City of Jerusalem after the Six Day War of 1967. Under his leadership the institute was renamed the 'Research Center of Kabbalah'.

In Paris, France, during the nineteen twenties and thirties the Armenian born philosopher, G.I. Gurdgieff, experimented with the techniques of Merkaba visualization . He had learned these methods in the course of his extensive travels throughout Central Asia and the Levant. He subsequently integrated them with a wide variety of Sufi dances and ritual movements.

During the nineteen forties and fifties the British pioneer of Analytical Psychology, Maurice Nicoll and his philosopher friend J.G. Bennett made some rather half-hearted attempts to integrate visualization techniques with other exercises. Nicoll was seduced and subsequently totally sidetracked by the new "pop" psychology of Jung, De Ropp, Laing, and Berne. Bennett, on the other hand was committed to finishing his *magnum opus*, "The Dramatic Universe". Because he had been sidetracked for several years by the *Subud* (an offshoot from the Naqshbandiya order of Dervishes) experience, he found himself unwilling, if not unable, to spend time and energy on integrating another dimension to his vision and already encyclopedic work, whether he believed it to be worthy or not.

In the nineteen sixties and seventies, interest in Kabbalah and the uses of visualization techniques, anything in fact that sounded mystical, however abstruse, reached new heights. The latest 'New Age" plethora of "Do it Yourself Universe Kits" surpassed anything that had gone before.

The nineteen eighties and nineties have brought us desktop computers and digitized images of ancient documents, previously inaccessible to the average researcher. It is interesting to note that Merkaba visualization methods have gained some measure of respectability through the writings of Charles Tart (*Waking Up*), and others. Successful results have been achieved in areas such as stress management, which have done much to accredit the general usefulness of such methods. Unfortunately, most of the techniques available today which claim a base in the Merkaba tradition have been built around fragments of the much earlier system, and tend to ignore the necessity for the accompanying physical and emotion related exercises.

Part Two

An Overview of Tarot Cards and Their Connections with Kabbalah

A set of Tarot cards קְלָפִים צִבְעוֹנִים (klafiim tzivoniim) consists of five groups of cards. The first four groups are collectively called the "Minor Arcana".

The suit of **Wands**	שרביטים	Fire	אש	World of Archetypes	עוֹלַם הָאֲצִילוּת
The suit of **Cups**	גביעים	Water	מים	World of Creation	עוֹלַם הַבְּרִיאָה
The suit of **Swords**	סיפים	Air	רוח	World of Formation	עוֹלַם הַיְצִירָה
The suit of **Pentacles**	מחמשים	Earth	עָפָר	World of Action	עוֹלַם הָעֲשִׂיָה

Each of these groups or suits contains ten Pip cards numbered one through ten קְלָפֵי הַסוּרִים (klafei HaSurim). Each suit also contains a number of Court cards קְלָפֵי תְמוּנוֹת (klafei timonot). In most modern sets of cards there are four Kings, four Queens, four Knights and four Pages. Thus the number of cards in each suit is Fourteen; making a total of fifty-six cards in the Minor Arcana. In order to complete the association with the Kabbalah and the ways of the Tree of life, we have chosen to return to a more ancient format which includes four Princesses, four Valets, and four Maids.

The fifth group of cards, the suit of trumps, is also known as the Major Arcana קְלָפִים הַנִּצְחוֹנִים (klafiim HaNitzkhonim) and contains twenty-two cards. The Middle Ages saw the progenitors of these cards developed and used as teaching devices by the numerous Muslims and Jews employed by the noble houses of an emerging Europe.

By the middle of the fourteenth century these pictorial "flash-cards" were being combined with the playing cards known in Spanish as *naipes*. There is strong evidence which suggests that this word derives from a Sanskrit word, *naib*, which was imported into early Arabic, and Hebrew as a generic name for playing cards. It is important to note that in Arabic, Aramaic, and Hebrew the root words for prophet and prophecy; *nabi*, *nabaa*, and *nevi* are possible roots for the Spanish *naipes*.

In Italy, Spain, and France of the Renaissance, the development of sophisticated games of chance and fortune telling methods using cards reached great heights. Numerous artists, many of them famous, were employed in the manufacture of Tarot cards. Until this time the cards we know as the Major Arcana were generally made without either numbers or titles, and the imagery varied considerably from country to country.

By the end of the nineteenth century it had become customary to number the cards of the Major Arcana, either from zero to twenty-one or from one to twenty-two. With the increase of interest in mysticism and the occult during the eighteenth and nineteenth centuries, each of these cards acquired a symbolic name, a magical title, and was assigned a letter of the Hebrew alphabet. This bias of the symbols towards a Jewish mystical interpretation occurred because of the parallel development of "Grimoires" (codices of mystical symbols associated with the study of Angelology).

Nobody really knows how, when or where Tarot and Tarot-like cards first developed. Were they a product of the East or the West? Were they developed as a game? For fortune telling? Or as P. D. Ouspensky (In Search of the Miraculous) suggests; contain some mysterious key to an ancient and long forgotten body of knowledge?

Certainly the twin shadows of Kabbalah and Sufism permeate the symbolism of the Tarot. Images of the Knights Templar rub shoulders with denizens of Greek mythology, and Torah is expounded by the Rosicrucians.

The format of this work is designed such that the attentive reader is invited to Examine, Explore and Enhance both the written and visual images. The reader is also encouraged to participate in the images, to create and recreate the building blocks of our circling thoughts, to begin the *Journey* of accessing and assessing the accumulated inner store of Wisdom, Understanding, and Knowledge.

Guide to the Paths on the Journey

1 ▷   STRENGTH   העצמה   ◁ 2

3 ▷   Path Eighteen   Chet ח   חית   נתיב השמונה עשרה   ◁ 4

5 ▷   Child of the Spinning Sword   ילד החרב המתהפכת   ◁ 6

God Called the Firmament Heaven   ◁ 7

המליך אות ח בראיה. וקשר לו כתר
תירוף זה בזה וצר בהם סרטן בעולם ותמוז
בשנה. ויד ימין בנפש זכר ונקבה.   ◁ 8

God made the letter Chet king over Sight and tied a crown
to it and combined them and from them made Cancer in the
Universe, Tammuz in the Year and the Right Hand in the Soul
Male and Female.   ◁ 9

The Awareness of Influx שכל בית השפע (*Sekhel Bet HaShefa*), so called because those who bind   ◁ 10
themselves to and serve this path receive certain mysterious substances and secrets directly from the Cause
of Causes.

Path Eighteen connects the Air part of the third sephira, Binah בינה (understanding) with the Fire part
of the sixth sephira, Tiferet תיפארת (beauty). It is the fifth and last of the paths that act as bridges   ◁ 11
across the abyss between the known and the unknown. Here we meet the real world in the zodiacal sign of
Cancer סרטן (sartan).

Samson is revealed after his long captivity. The former Nazarite destroys the Portal of the Philistine
temple at Gaza. The balustrade, friezes, parochet and columns crumble before his God.   ◁ 12
Emboldened by his fantasy of conquest, the Charioteer seems poised for action.

We are in the captivity of the mysteries of the Philistine. We are surrounded by distractions
from the purpose of our journey.

On the threshold between the sacred and the profane, we seek the strength and the wisdom
to liberate our spirituality from the bonds of the World of Action and to propel us into the   ◁ 13
World To Come (*Olam Ha-Ba*).

Only after the humiliation of deceit, captivity, desolation and blindness does he become
cognizant of the strength within.

Like Samson we must learn from this vision to avoid the dangers and distractions of the
foreign environments in which we live.

---

1. Standard English Title
2. Standard Hebrew Title
3. Path number per the *Sefer Yetzirah* with the traditionally ascribed Hebrew letter
4. Hebrew translations of number three
5. Alternative English Title for the Path
6. Alternative Hebrew Title for the Path
7. The link between the thirty-two paths of the Tree of Life and the thirty-two actions of God in the first chapter of Genesis
8. The verse from the *Sefer Yetzirah* which refers to the letter of the Hebrew Alphabet
9. English translation of number eight
10. The aspect of our "consciousness" attributes to the Path and a short commentary derived from the *Sefer Yetzirah* and the *Bahir*
11. The correspondence of the Path with Astrological symbolism
12. A general description of the illustration
13. A meditation based on the symbolism of the Path

The first group of paths within the Tree of Life

Emanating from the sephira Keter כתר, they are as follows

א   The Magician,   ב   The High Priestess and   ג   the Empress

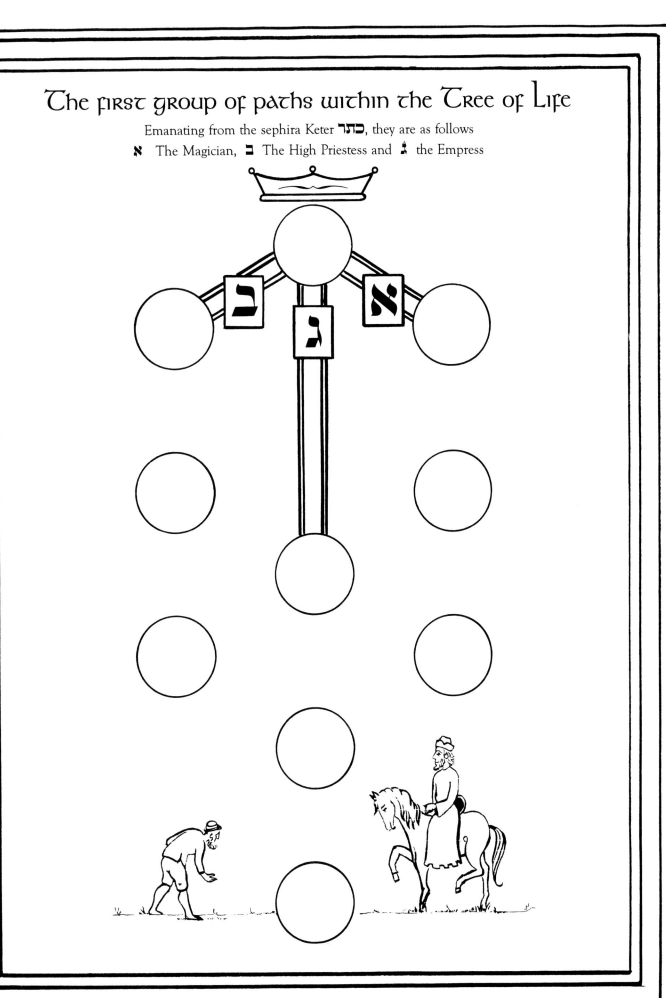

The Magician  המכשף

Path Eleven   Aleph   א   נתיב האחת עשרה   אלף
The Magus of Power   אשף העצמה
God made the Firmament

המליך אות א' ברוח וקשר לו כתר
וצרפן זה בזה יצר בהם אויר בעולם ורויה בשנה
וגויה בנפש זכר באמ"ש ונקבה באש"ים

God made the letter Aleph king over the Breath and bound
a crown to it and combined them. With them, God made Air in
the universe, Abundance in the year and a torso in the soul:
the male with AMSh the female with AShM.

The Polished Awareness שכל המצוחצח (Sekhel HaMetzutzakh), so called because it contains the hidden source of the Abyss שאול (sheol) between the known and the unknown and the veil before the Ark of the Torah; constantly reflecting and returning our worldly encumbrances to us.

Path Eleven combines all the Air signs: Libra מאזנים (maznayim), Aquarius דלי (deli) and Gemini תאומים (taumim). It encompasses each of the Qualities: Evolving, Maintaining and Transforming. Path Eleven connects the Earth part of the first sephira, Keter כתר, (the crown) with the Fire part of the second sephira, Hokhmah חכמה (wisdom).

The Magician stands between the Earth and the Sky, his garments decorated with the signs and symbols of the planets and of the Zodiac. In one hand he holds a wand; symbol of Fire, with one end pointed towards the sky. The other hand holds the scales of Libra and indicates the Earth spread out before him. Nearby stands a cup, symbol of the powers of Water and a sword, symbolic of the powers of Air.

The Magician's face is radiant and full of confidence; his hands play the elemental signs like instruments in an ethereal orchestra. Each action is full of significance. Each new combination of the symbols creates unending cascades of unexpected phenomena.

Watching this ceaseless flow of events we are forced to inquire, "For whom is all this theater? Where is the audience?" An echo of our question seems to reply, saying, "Is an audience really necessary? Observe."

Again we look at the Magician and see innumerable crowds passing to and fro within him, disappearing from view as we perceive them. Reflecting on this we see that the Magician and Audience are one and the same.

Through the Magician's eyes we see ourselves and each other in him, reflected as in a mirror. At the same time we know that there is nothing before us but the blue sky and the memory of a window opening within us; through which we have seen unworldly things and heard unworldly sounds.

The Magus of Power

The High Priestess   כהנת הגדולה

Path Twelve   Bet   ב   בית   נתיב השתים עשרה

Priestess of the Star   כהנת הכוכב

God Saw That the Light Was Good

המליך אות ב׳ בחכמה וקשר לו כתר
וצרפן זה בזה וצר בהם לבנה בעולם יום ראשון
בשנה ועין ימין בנפש זכר ונקבה

God made the letter Bet king over Wisdom and bound a crown to it and
combined them. With them, God made the Moon in the universe, The
first weekday (all Sundays) in the year and a Right Eye in the soul:
Male and Female

The **Bright Awareness** שכל הבהיר (*Sekhel HaBahir*), so called because it is the seat of the great prophetess and the powers of the Auphanim ופנים (wheels). It is also the source of the visions of those who seek divine ecstasy.

Path Twelve connects the Air part of the first sephira, Keter כתר (crown) with the Fire part of the third Sephira, Binah בינה (understanding). Our perceptions of exploration and of work on this path are affected by the cycles and rhythms of the planet Mercury כוכב (*cochav*) and its aspectual circle.

The entrance to the outer court of the Temple is guarded by great pillars. The High Priestess stands before us, her garments all the colors of the night sky swirling around her. Between the pillars hangs a veil decorated with pomegranates and grapes, symbolizing the fruits of the World to Come. The pillars are a reminder that Torah is the first requirement of the seeker on the path.

As our awareness grows, a curtain parts and we approach the woman veiled in the half darkness.

The Mystery of Mysteries filled her. She was at once the High Priestess, the Prophetess, the Wise Woman, the Wife, the Lover, the Mother and the Daughter.

Rampant lions symbolize both physical and spiritual strength. They are the Guardians of Scholarship. The Pillars become *etzei haim* (Torah staves) and the ripe fruits reveal the wonders of the Law.

Her beauty transcends all definitions of human boundaries. The High Priestess writes mystic symbols on her pale skin which instantly and endlessly transform from one language to another; gradually disappearing into the endless flow which the symbols themselves have inaugurated.

We have been awakened to the possibilities of understanding.

This understanding, as it encounters the accrued wisdom of the Magician allows us into the world of real knowledge.

PRIESTESS OF THE STAR

The Empress

הַקֵיסָרִית

Path Thirteen   Gimel   ג

נתיב השלשה עשר גימל

Daughter of the Titans

בת הנפילים

God saw that it was good

המליך אות ג' בעושר וקשר לו כתר
וצרפן זה בזה וצר בהם מאדים בעולם יום שני
בשנה ואזן ימין בנפש זכר ונקבה

God made the letter Gimel king over Abundance and tied a crown to it and combined them. With them God made Mars in the Universe, the second day (all Mondays) in the year and the Right Ear in the Soul: Male and Female.

The Directing Awareness שכל מנהיג האחדות (*Sekhel Manhig HaAkhdut*), so called because its glory is the vessel containing the essence of unified spirituality.

Path Thirteen is the first of the bridges traversing the Abyss שאול (*sheol*). It connects the Earth part of the first sephira, Keter כתר (the crown); with the Fire part of the sixth sephira, Tiferet תפארת (beauty). The cycles of the Moon ירח (*yereakh*) and its aspectual circle govern the manifestations of this path in the world of actions.

The Empress is seated securely on her strongly built Throne. Her calm face belies the intensity of her gaze which penetrates and passes through us. She is framed by a dense shrubbery, symbolic of the fruits of all of the possible Worlds to Come.

The scent of flowers, countless singing birds, the exuberance of spring and universal renewal are upon us. All the potentials of all the worlds are present in her fertile glance. Wherever her gaze penetrates, worlds are created and buds unfold.

The twelve stars of her crown await their realization in the world as the precious gems which adorn the breastplates of the High Priest.

Her garment is shocking in the intensity of its vibrant red clay coloring and austere lines. We ask ourselves, "Is this the Fire of the Earth or is it perhaps the Earth of the Fire?"
The sweetness she imparts to the world is seen in the beautiful flowers which beckon us forward.

We come to understand that the Empress provides The Power which is defined by the High Priestess and administered in the World of Actions by the Four Queens of the third sephira, Binah (Understanding).

Daughter of the Titans

The second group of Paths within the Tree of Life

Emanating from the second sephira Hochmah חכמה, they are as follows:

ד The Emperor, ה The High Priest and ו the Lovers

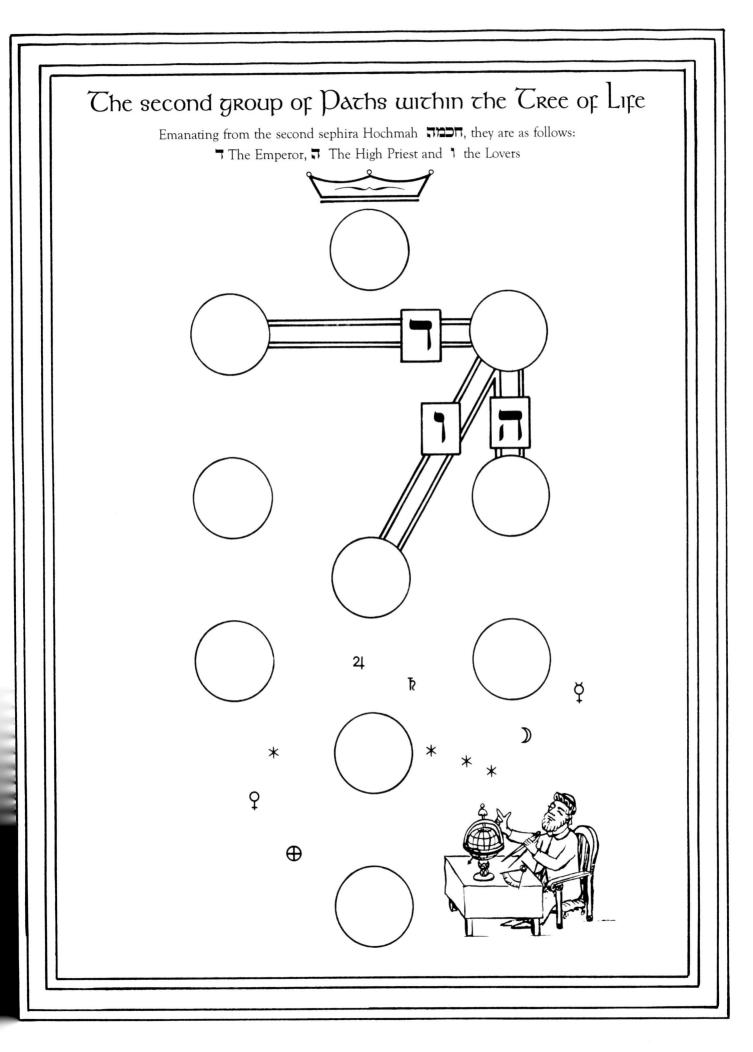

The Emperor   הקיסר

Path Fourteen   Dalet   ד   דל'ת   נתיב הארבע עשרה

Lord of the Dawn   אדיר שמש הבקר

God Saw That It Was Good

המליך אות ד' בזרע וקשר לו כתר
וצרפן זה בזה וצר בהם חמה בעולם יום שלישי
בשנה ונחיר ימין בנפש זכר ונקבה

God made the letter Dalet king over Seed and fastened a crown
to it and combined them. With them, God made the Sun in the
universe, the Third Day (all Tuesdays) in the year and the
Right Nostril in the Soul: Male and Female

The Illuminated Awareness שכל המאיר (*Sekhel HaMeyir*), so called because it contains the source of the Silent Speech of the Angels which transports light into darkness and sound into silence.

Path Fourteen connects the Water part of the second sephira, Hochmah חכמה (wisdom) with the Water part of the third sephira, Binah בינה (understanding). Our ability to travel this path is formalized by working with the cycles of the planet Venus נוגה (*nogah*) and its aspectual circle.

The Emperor, like the Empress, is seated securely on his throne. A richly made canopy is above him. The luxuriant shrubbery is symbolic of the earthly domains that he rules. His robe, like that of the Empress is symbolic of the power of the World of Fire in the World of Earth. This power is expressed in the World through the actions of the four Kings of the second sephira חכמה (*Hochmah*).

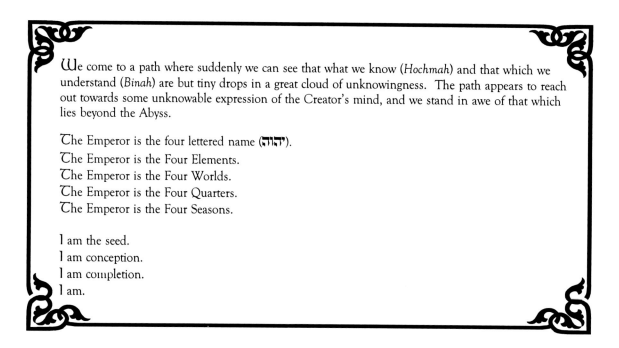

We come to a path where suddenly we can see that what we know (*Hochmah*) and that which we understand (*Binah*) are but tiny drops in a great cloud of unknowingness. The path appears to reach out towards some unknowable expression of the Creator's mind, and we stand in awe of that which lies beyond the Abyss.

The Emperor is the four lettered name (יהוה).
The Emperor is the Four Elements.
The Emperor is the Four Worlds.
The Emperor is the Four Quarters.
The Emperor is the Four Seasons.

I am the seed.
I am conception.
I am completion.
I am.

LORD of the Dawn

The High Priest   הכהן הגדול

Path Fifteen   Heh   ה   נתיב החמש עשרה הא

Lord of Eternity   רבון עולמי עד

The Spirit of God Hovered

המליך אות ה׳ בשיחה וקשר לו כתר
וצרפן זה בזה וצר בהם טלה בעולם
וניסן בשנה ורגל ימין בנפש זכר ונקבה

God made the letter Heh king over Speech and fixed a crown to it
and combined them. With them, God made Aries in the Universe,
Nisan in the Year and the Right Foot in the soul:
Male and Female.

The Supporting Awareness שכל המעמיד (*Sekhel HaMa-amid*), so called because it acts as the base or platform דוכן (*dukhan*) on which the Act of Creation is balanced against the charged foreboding of Sinai. "Gloom is its Crown ." (Job 35:9)

Path Fifteen connects the Earth part of the second sephira, Hochmah חכמה (wisdom) with the Fire part of the fourth sephira, Chesed חסד (grace). It is the second of the five paths which act as bridges across the abyss between the known and the unknown. All new beginnings have their roots in this path. Here the High Priest meets the Vernal Equinox in the zodiacal sign of the Ram טלה (*taaleh*).

"These are the Vestments they shall make: a Breastplate and an Ephod, a Robe, a pattern-woven Tunic, a Turban and a Sash. They shall make them as Sacred Garments for Aaron and his sons so that they may be priests to Me. Artisans shall take the Gold, the Sky Blue, the Dark Red and the Crimson Wool and the Linen and fashion them into garments." (Exodus 28:4-5.)

The High Priest stands at the Pulpit which is before the great pillars of the Temple.
He seems to beckon to us, one hand half raised in the priestly blessing, the other holding a censer filled with the allure of sweet smelling spices, perfumes and incense.

Our questions seem to fade and become enveloped in the enormous silence of the Presence. We hear the sounds of his voice but fail to understand the words; either we are ignorant of the language or something unknowable prevents our comprehension. As our attention focuses in the silence, a small echo of our own voices provides answers for those of us who have ears to hear.

Do not hear what He does not say.
Do not believe you hear before you have really heard.
Do not put your words in the place of His words.

This Is Our Key To The True State Of Grace Required For Proper Beginnings And For Continuity In The World.

LORD OF ETERNITY

The Lovers האהובים

Path Sixteen   Vav   ו   וו נתיב הששׁ עשׂרה

Children of the Voice   ילדי הדבר

God divided between the Light and the Darkness

המליך אות ו׳ בבהרהור וקשׁר לו כתר
וצרפן זה בזה וצר בהם שׁור בעולם ואייר בשׁנה
וכוליא ימנית בנפשׁ זכר ונקבה

God made the letter Vav king over Thought and tied a crown
to it and combined them. With them, God made Taurus in the
Universe, Iyar in the Year and the
Right Kidney in the Soul: Male and Female.

The Enduring Awareness שכל הנצחי (*Sekhel HaNitzchi*), so called because it is the Garden of Eden עדן גן (*gan edan*) prepared as a reward for the Saints. No direct Glory exists at a lower level than this path except as reflection or refraction.

Path Sixteen connects the Air part of the second sephira, Hochmah חכמה (wisdom) with the Fire part of the sixth sephira, Tiferet תפארת (beauty). It is the third of the five paths which act as bridges across the abyss between the known and the unknown. Creation and creativity have their beginnings in this path. Here the Lovers are betrothed in the zodiacal sign of Taurus, the Bull שׁור (*shor*).

The Wedding Canopy is symbolic of the fulfillment of the Creator's hopes for Spiritual and Temporal union. It is decorated with pomegranates which remind us of both the obligations to the Law and the fecundity of the forthcoming union. As the betrothal period comes to an end, the Bride and Groom stand under the Chuppah bedecked in finery.

As we near the Great City our attention is drawn to a colorful spectacle.

The solid stone and brick of the fortifications fades from our view as the marital couple are revealed under the *Chuppah*. They have eyes only for one another and their gaze fixes on a place unseen by us.

The Chuppah is supported by the trunks of trees planted at their births by their parents. As they join the circle of life, they stand poised with their Tree held ready for planting.

By plotting their troth they have joined in a spiritual union that radiates about them and connects them to the World of Action in the Bridal Chamber which lies beyond our sight.

It takes our breath away to see such beauty and completion.

We can only hope that on our journey we will recognize the resolve which binds them together.

Children of the Voice

The third group of paths within the Tree of Life

Emanating from the third sephira Binah בינה, they are as follows:

ז The Chariot and ח Strength

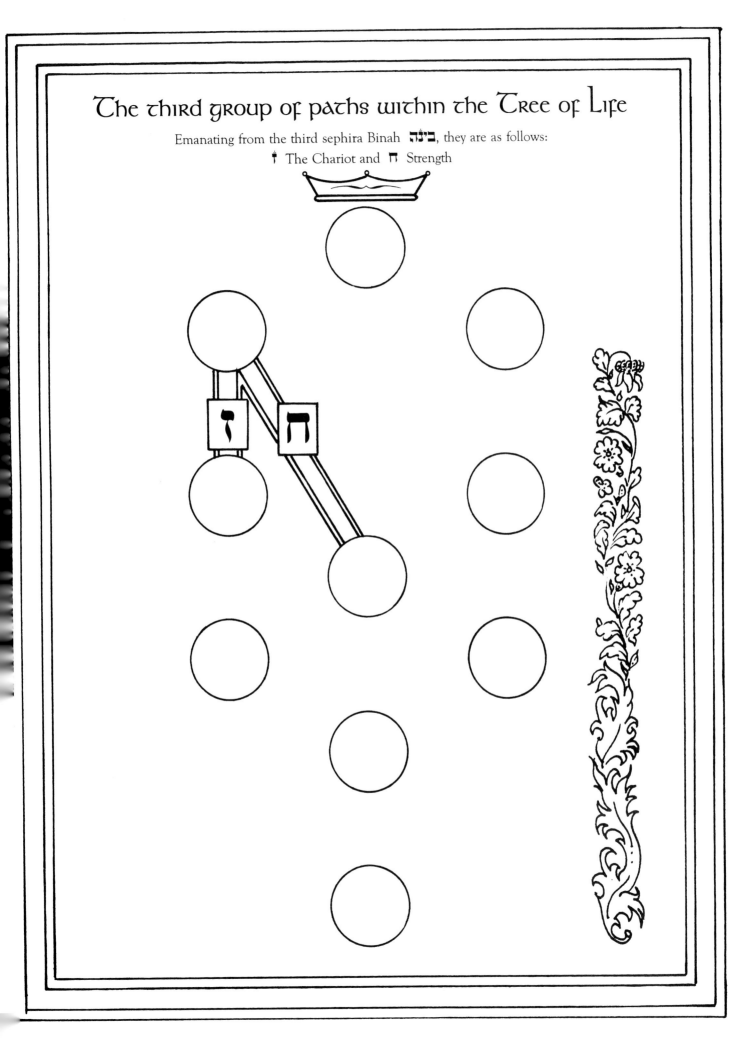

The Chariot   המרכבה

Path Seventeen   Zayin   ז   נתיב השבע עשרה   זין

Triumph of Light   נצחון האור

God Called the Light Day

המליך אות ז׳ בהלוך וקשר לו כתר
וצרפן זה בזה וצר בהם תאומים בעולם וסיון
בשנה ורגל שמאל בנפש זכר ונקבה

God made the letter Zayin king over Motion and tied
a crown to it and combined them. From them God created
Gemini in the universe, Sivan in the year, the Left Foot
in the soul: Male and Female.

The Sensory Awareness שכל ההרגש (Sekhel HaHargash), called thus because it provides the means for the Saints and the Faithful to perceive and appreciate the spiritual clothing of holiness and The Way.

Path Seventeen connects the Earth part of the third sephira, Binah בינה (understanding) with the Fire part of the fifth sephira, Gevurah גבורה (strength). It is the fourth of the five paths that act as bridges across the abyss between the known and the unknown. Here the Charioteer meets the roots of new ideas and formulations arising in the zodiacal sign of Gemini תאומים (taumim).

The Traveler has transformed himself into the Conqueror and the Vanquished. He stands on a conveyance that he can barely direct. The Chariot is propelled by his limited ability to maintain the tension between the understanding of how it moves and his ability to effect control. The eyes await a moment of weakness so that they might direct themselves away from the City of his Aspirations.

Emboldened by his fantasy of conquest, the Charioteer seems poised for action.

We ask him 'Where are you going, over whom do you seek dominion?'
Our answer remains in the silence. He is a legend only in his mind.

Unable to distract his energies for even a moment, he focuses intently upon his mission.

We know that he will never reach his destination. The ability to see beyond the now is impeded by his task.

His weapons are useless, regardless of the inherent power each contains.

Without understanding that the wheels of the Chariot can show him the totality of knowledge and sight, he will wander ceaselessly through Eternity.

The Triumph of Light

STRENGTH הֶעָצְמָה

Path Eighteen   Chet   ח   חית   נתיב השמונה עשרה

Child of the Spinning Sword   ילד החרב המתהפכת

God Called the Firmament Heaven

המליך אות ח' בראיה וקשר לו כתר
וצרפן זה בזה וצר בהם סרטן בעולם ותמוז
בשנה ויד ימין בנפש זכר ונקבה

God made the letter Chet king over Sight and tied a crown
to it and combined them and from them made Cancer in the
Universe, Tammuz in the Year and the Right Hand in the Soul:
Male and Female.

The Awareness of Influx שׂכל בית השׁפע (Sekhel Bet HaShefa), so called because those who bind themselves to and serve this path receive certain mysterious substances and secrets directly from the Cause of Causes.

Path Eighteen connects the Air part of the third sephira, Binah בינה (understanding) with the Fire part of the sixth sephira, Tiferet תפארת (beauty). It is the fifth and last of the paths that act as bridges across the abyss between the known and the unknown. Here we meet the real world in the zodiacal sign of Cancer סרטן (sartan).

Samson is revealed after his long captivity. The former Nazarite destroys the Portal of the Philistine temple at Gaza. The balustrade, friezes, parochet and columns crumble before his God.
Emboldened by his fantasy of conquest, the Charioteer seems poised for action.

We are in the captivity of the mysteries of the Philistine. We are surrounded by distractions from the purpose of our journey.

On the threshold between the sacred and the profane, we seek the strength and the wisdom to liberate our spirituality from the bonds of the World of Action and to propel us into the World To Come (Olam Ha-Ba).

Only after the humiliation of deceit, captivity, desolation and blindness does he become cognizant of the strength within.

Like Samson we must learn from this vision to avoid the dangers and distractions of the foreign environments in which we live.

Child of the Spinning Sword

The fourth group of paths within the Tree of Life

Emanating from the fourth sephira Chesed חסד they are as follows:

ט The Hermit, י The Wheel of Fortune and כ Justice

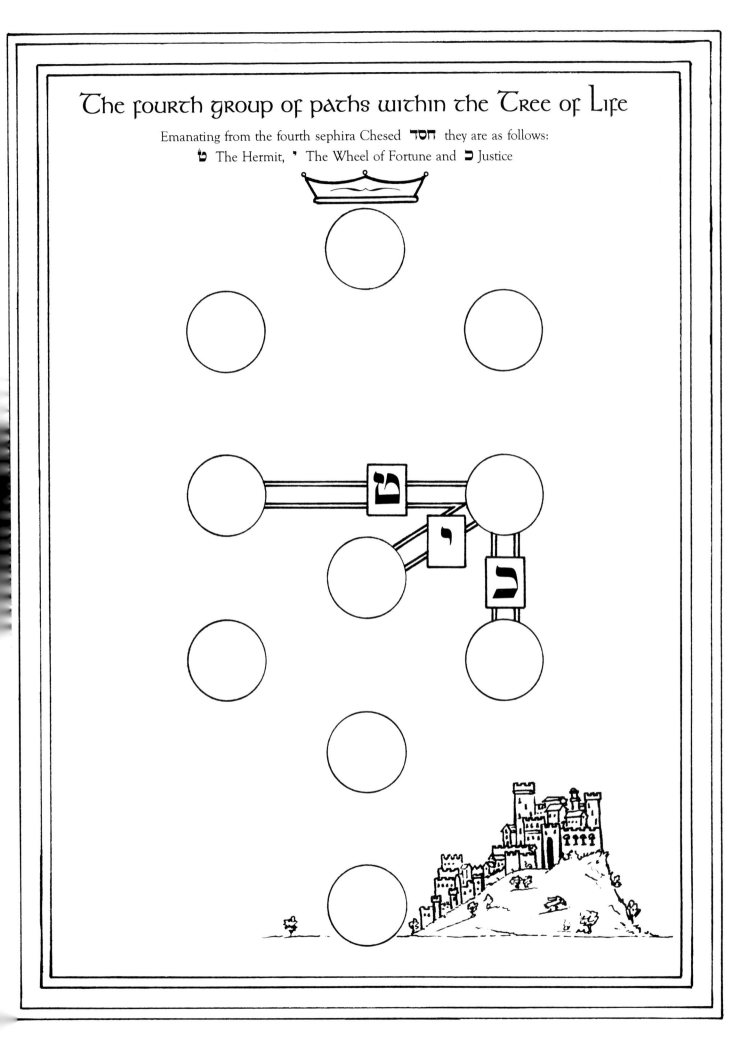

The Hermit   הַנָּזִיר

Path Nineteen   Tet   ט   טית   נתיב התשעה עשרה

Promise of the Eternal   ברית האינסופי

God called the dry land Earth

המליך אות ט׳ בשמיעה וקשר לו כתר
וצרפן זה בזה וצר בהם אריה בעולם ואב
בשנה כוליא שמאלית בנפש זכר ונקבה

God made the letter Tet king over Hearing and bound a
crown to it and combined them. With them God formed Leo in
the universe, Av in the year and the Left Kidney in the soul:
Male and Female

The **Spiritual Awareness** שכל המעמיד (*Sekhel HaMaamid*) consolidates the emanations of the higher powers; balances them and provides access to the lower paths.

Path Nineteen connects the Water part of the fourth sephira, Chesed חסד (grace) with the Water part of the fifth sephira, Gevurah גבורה (strength). It contains the zodiacal sign of Leo אריה (*aryeh*). It allows Grace to temper our Strength so that we may gain equilibrium in our Spiritual Life.

The Hermit's regal demeanor seems inappropriate in the harsh surroundings of the wilderness. The acacia tree in the distance indicates a hidden source of water. The staff is alive with the thirty-two paths of the Tree of Life. The serpent loses his opportunity to strike.

Our Chariot has taken us to a place far from the familiar. We cleanse ourselves, body, soul and mind of all preconceived notions, We come alone to the presence of God.

The Hermit beckons to the snake, "Come. I will give you the answers you seek. Your exile from Eden is over, I carry my light within and without; its radiance pierces the glow of morning. All is revealed to me, but my journey prevents me from reaching my goal.

I meditate on all of God's creations with equal zeal. All things brought before me are one with God, and reflect both Strength and Grace.

My staff springs forth verdant from the bareness and desolation. Life is revealed in the harshness of solitude.

Only on this path will I find the reality of the Almighty in my heart."

Promise of the Eternal

WHEEL OF FORTUNE

גלגל המזל

Path Twenty   Yod   י   נתיב העשרים   יוד

Master of Force   רבון הכוח

God placed them in the Firmament

המליך אות י' במעשה וקשר לו כתר
וצרפן זה בזה וצר בהם בתולה בעולם ואלול
בשנה ויד שמאל בנפש זכר ונקבה

God made the letter Yod king over action and tied a crown
to it and combined them. From them God formed Virgo in the
universe Elul in the year and the Left Hand in the soul:
Male and Female

The Awareness of Will שכל הרצון (*Sekhel HaRatzon*), so called because it contains the structural elements from which the World of Formation עולם היצירה (*Olam HaYetzirah*) is built.

Path Twenty connects the Air part of the fourth sephira, Chesed חסד (grace) with the Fire part of the sixth sephira, Tiferet תפארת (beauty). The zodiacal sign of Virgo בתולה (*betula*) is contained by this path and our Emotional perceptions are moderated by the cycles of the forces contained in this sign.

At the edge of the desert where the Hermit roams, people live out their daily existence unaware that the Wheel of Fortune; the totality of existence in the universe, plunges inexorably through the time and space that it creates. Lives are carried in the moment and there is little awareness of placement in the universal continuum.

The Eternal Circle of Life approaches.

All that is born, dies; all that is, was, and all of Creation exists within the zodiacal circumference.

Set on its journey into perpetuity by Angels creating time and space, its constancy is symbolic of Eternity.

Knowledge of our transience in the universe intrudes on our limited awareness.

Slowly we perceive the multitude of paths which are constantly before us.

We struggle to maintain our hold and follow into the Forever, but our grasp cannot exceed our reach.

Master of Force

JUSTICE   שׁוֹפְטוֹת

Path Twenty-one   Caph   כ   כף   נתיב העשרים ואחד

Daughter of Truth   בת האמת

God saw that it was good

המליך אות כ' בחיים וקשר לו כתר
וצרפן זה בזה וצר בהם נוגה בעולם יום רביעי
בשנה ועין שמאל בנפש זכר ונקבה

God made the letter Caph king over Life and tied a crown
to it and combined them; from them God formed Venus in the
universe, Wednesdays in the year and the Left Eye in the soul:
Male and Female.

The **Desired Awareness** שכל החפץ (*Sekhel HaChafetz*), so called because it contains the divine seed of our emotions as they are expressed in the World of Action through the seventh sephira, Netzach נצח (victory).

Path Twenty-one connects the Earth part of the fourth sephira, חסד (grace) with the Fire part of the seventh sephira נצח (victory). Our everyday feelings become charged with all the power of our latent emotional energies which are governed on this path by the aspectual circle of the planet Jupiter.

We see before us the Sword and Scales of Justice suspended in space and time. Beyond these two great symbols lies the Eternal City, Zion. Above all rises a Canopy; the blue coloring reminds us of the creation of the Heavens and of the Waters of Life.

The Sword is that which guards the Garden of Eden and the way of the Tree of Life.

The Scales remind us of imagery in the Jewish High Holiday liturgy in which human deeds are weighed by God. The Fate of creation and its inhabitants hangs in the balance at this time of year.

Appoint yourselves judges and guards for your tribes in all your settlements which God your Lord is giving you, and be certain that they administer honest judgment for your people.

Do not bend Justice and do not give anyone special consideration. Do not take bribes, since bribery makes the wise blind and perverts the words of the righteous. Pursue perfect honesty, in order that you might live and occupy the land which God your Lord is giving to you.

Deuteronomy 16: 18-20

Daughter of Truth

The fifth group of paths within the Tree of Life

Emanating from the fifth sephira Gevurah גברה they are as follows:

ל The Hanged Man and מ Death

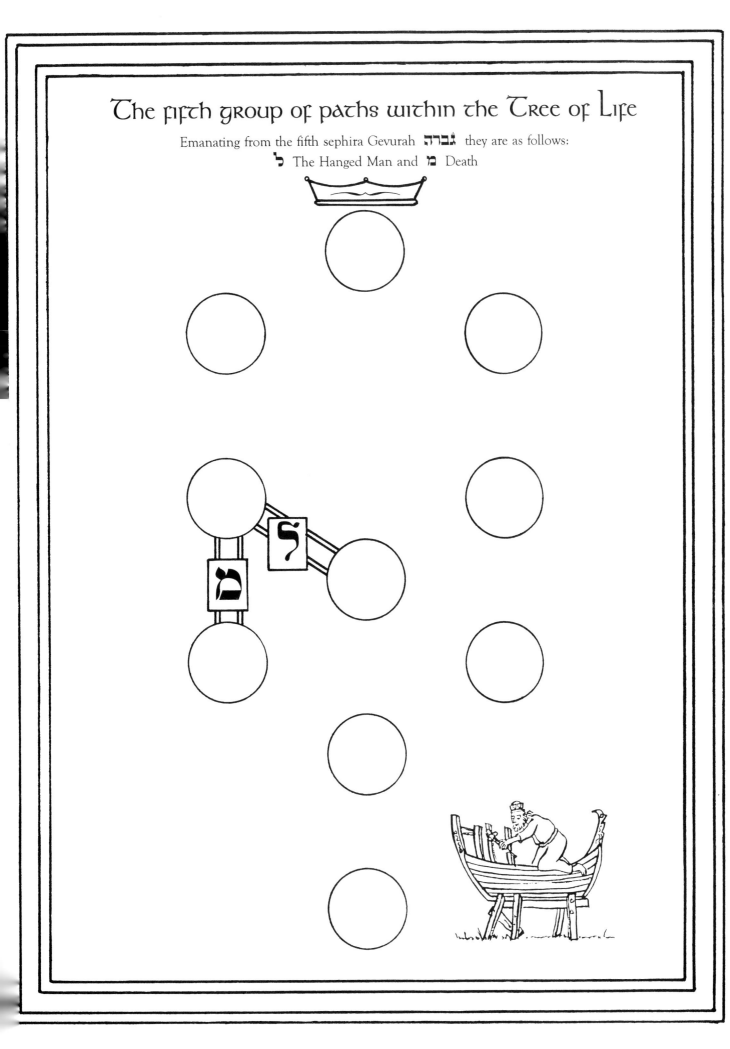

The Hanged Man   התלוי

Path Twenty-two   Lamed   ל   למד   נתיב עשרים ושתים

Spirit of the Endless Waters   רוח מים האינסופי

God Created Great Whales

המליך אות ל׳ בתשמיש וקשר לו כתר
וצרפן זה בזה וצר בהם מאזנים בעולם ותשרי
בשנה ומרה בנפש זכר ונקבה

God made the letter Lamed king over Procreation and tied
a crown to it and combined them; from them God made Libra in the
Universe, Tishri in the year and a Gall Bladder in the soul:
Male and Female

The Faithful Awareness שׂכל הנאמן (*Sekhel HaNe-aman*), so called because spiritual awareness, growth, power and endurance are enhanced by the work done on this path.

Path Twenty-two connects the Air part of the fifth sephira Gevurah גבורה (strength), with the Fire part of the sixth sephira Tiferet תפארת (beauty). As we travel this Path our natural responses to the environment are greatly affected by the rhythms and cycles which are contained in the zodiacal sign of Libra מאזנים (*maznaim*), which is defined by this path.

The Hanged Man is suspended by some unseen force from a gallows built from living trees. His head is surrounded by a halo of flames which reminds us of the radiance of God's presence in Moses. Beyond him we see the City filled with sunshine and life, seemingly unaware of the dramatic moment before our eyes.

We hang suspended between the Tree of Life and The Tree of Knowledge;

And see the Truth.

Our Journey is without end, we pass from initiation to initiation, from failure to success.

We are the Magician controlling the elements and the one who walks the path of the Fool.

We are all of those who are between, and more.

The Abyss is always before us and the Serpent always awaits us in the desert.

In Zion we find the Truth, Constancy and everlasting Companionship.

SPIRIT OF THE ENDLESS WATERS

Death   המות

Path Twenty-three   Mem   מ   מם   נתיב עשרים ושלוש

The Great Transformer   רבון השנוי

God Made Two Lights

המליך אות מ' במים וקשר לו כתר
וצרפן זה בזה וצר בהם ארץ בעולם וקור בשנה
ובטן בנפש זכר במא''ש ונקבה במש''א

God made the letter Mem king over Water and tied a crown
to it and combined them. From them God made the Earth in
the universe, Cold in the year and a Stomach in the Soul:
The male with שׁאמ the female with אשׁמ

The Sustaining Awareness שכל הקים (Sekhel HaKayam), so called because it contains the qualities necessary for releasing the energy which sustains the continuing existence of the sephirot in the World of Action.

Path Twenty-three connects the Earth part of the fifth sephira, Gevurah גבורה (strength) with the Fire part of the eighth sephira, Hod הוד (splendor). The Twenty-third Path contains all three water signs, Cancer סרטן (sartan), Pisces דגים (dagim), and Scorpio עקרב (akrav). As we travel this path we encounter forces which may misdirect us. Imagination and Inspiration are the fruits of work on this path.

We have wandered deeper into the desert where we met the Hermit with his lamp, and saw the endless turning of the Wheel of Life. The crowned skeletal figure of Death stands before us wielding a large scythe. His glance is ominous, but, as our vision clears and we see that the handle of the scythe is the Tree of Life, it turns to one of amusement.

The Great Transformer stands at the edge of the dusty desert reaping his bounty.

"What is Death?" we asked.

The Great Transformation awaits you.

We rest briefly on our journey, closing our eyes seeking respite from the glare.

The Transformer continues the relentless and eternal task of re-creation of the essences of all that lives in the world, and re-distributing it into worlds which lie beyond our vision.

"Have we reached the end of our journey?"

In all that is living there is death. And in death lies the promise of rebirth. Our Way continues forever, sometimes in the light and sometimes seeking rest and renewal in the darkness. The Tree of Life continues to support us through all of the planes of our continued existence.

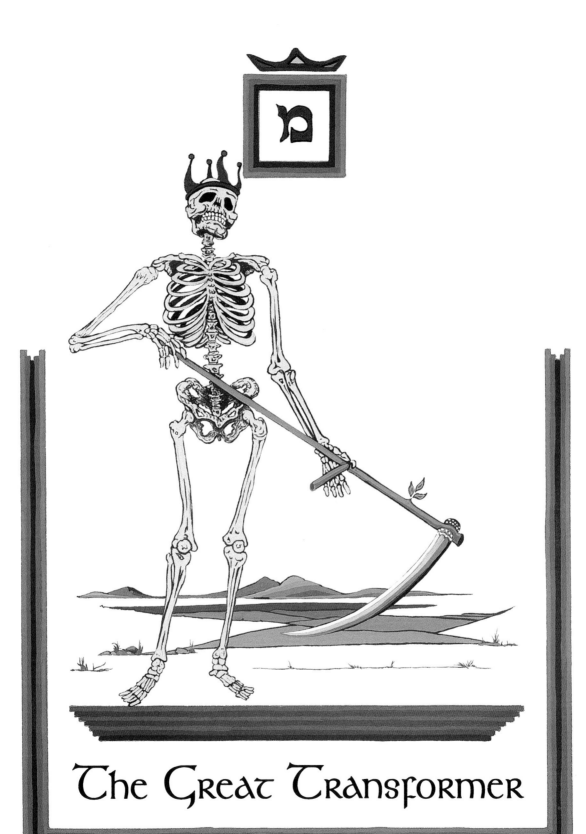

The Great Transformer

The sixth group of paths within the Tree of Life

Emanating from the sixth sephira Tiferet תפארת they are as follows:

נ Temperance ס The Devil and ע The Tower

TEMPERANCE מתימות

Path Twenty-four   Nun   נ   נן   נתיב העשרים וארבע

Spirit of Life   רוח הַחיים

God Blessed Them

המליך אות נ' בריח וקשר לו כתר
וצרפן זה בזה וצר בהם עקרב בעולם וחשון
בשנה ודקין בנפש זכר ונקבה

God made the letter Nun king over smell and tied a crown
to it and combined them. With them, God made Scorpio in
the Universe, Heshvan in the Year and the Intestine in the Soul:
Male and Female

The Imagining Awareness שכל הדמיוני (Sekhel HaDimioni) so called because it provides us with paradigms for all creative phenomena in a form appropriate to their place in the Universe.

Path Twenty-four brings the essence of the sixth sephira Tiferet תפארת (beauty) into that part of the world of our senses defined by the seventh sephira Netzach נצח (victory). The expression of activity on this path is one of Feelings rather than of Thought and is said to be enhanced by virtue of actions occurring under the governance of the zodiacal sign of Scorpio עקרב (akrav).

The Heavenly messenger stands with feet placed firmly in the world. The Angelic power transforms the contents of the goblets. The number of the wing's large outer feathers alludes to the number of the ways of the Tree of Life. Within the protective orb of the wings we find the Two hundred and Thirty-one gates of Israel through which the rest of the world was created.

Although the Angel roams free in the universe, above and below, here feet are firmly planted on the ground. What keeps the angel here is the need to complete the Work. When it is finished, the Angel will be re-united with The Almighty. The task is never-ending. Mortal time can not comprehend. It cannot escape.

The angel has turned away from us since we seem not to understand. Day and night, past and future, right and wrong, male and female flow back and forth. The giving and taking of the water of life creates an endless sparkling flow of all the colors of the rainbow as it passes through time and space anticipating the Creation.

Balance is critical, a step one way or another will send us reeling into an excess of thoughts and feelings and ultimately, oblivion.

The Angel indicates the path that the Chariot should take towards the unified revelation of self as Torah.

SPIRIT OF LIFE

The Devil   יצר הרע

Path Twenty-five   Samech   ס   סמך   נתיב העשרים וחמשה

Father of Lies   הַשָּׂטָן

God Created Man

המליך אות ס׳ בבשׂינה וקשׁר לו כתר
וצרפן זה בזה וצר בהם קשׁת בעולם
וכסלו בשׁנה קבה בנפשׁ זכר ונקבה

God made the letter Samech king over Sleep and bound a crown to it
and combined them. With them, God made Sagittarius in the Universe,
Kislev in the Year and Digestion in the soul:
Male and Female.

The Experimenting Awareness שׂכל הנסיוני (*Sekhel HaNisioni*), so called because it contains the elements of the original temptation; symbolically represented by the story of the Garden of Eden, through which God tests all of his saints, the sages, and other creatures made in God's image.

Path Twenty-five connects the Air part of the sixth sephira Tiferet תפארת (beauty) with the Fire part of the eighth sephira Hod הוד (splendor). It contains all of the zodiacal sign of Sagittarius קשׂת (*keshet*), and all of the forces resident in that sign affect our workings on that path.

The Devil stands before us, ready to pounce upon our slightest weakness. The membranous wings stretch out seeking to encompass the entire sky.

Once more we leave the seemingly safe surroundings of the city of our thoughts

All that has come before was illusion.

We have found no balance, no flow that perpetuates the Truth from realm to realm.

There is no reality without the lie, and there is no lie without reality.

Weakness of the spirit, lack of resolve and clarity of the mind are inevitable.

We struggle to see past the ominous beating of the wings hoping to catch a glimpse of the world to come and perhaps to regain our foothold on the path.

"Beyond Me lies the Garden of Certainty which you seek."

Beyond the dangers of the claws that beckon.

FATHER OF LIES

The Tower המגדל

Path Twenty-Six   Ayin   ע   עין   ושש   העשרים   נתיב

House of Illusion   בית טעות החושים

In the Form of God, He Created Him

המליך אות ע' בברוגז וקשר לו כתר

וצרפן זה בזה וצר בהם גדי בעולם

וטבת בשנה וכבד בנפש זכר ונקבה

God made the letter Ayen king over Anger and bound a crown to it and
made them one. With them, God made Capricorn in the Universe,
Tevet in the Year and the Liver in the soul:
the Male and the Female

The Renewing Awareness שכל המחדש (*Sekhel HaMechudash*), so called because it contains the means
that God uses to channel new things into the World of Creation.

Path Twenty-six connects the Earth part of the sixth sephira Tiferet תפארת (beauty) with the Fire part of
the ninth sephira Yesod יסוד (foundation). All of the natural cycles touching the zodiacal sign of Capricorn
גדי (*gdi*) are renewed on this path.

The Tower of Babel מגדל בבל (*migdal bavel*) strains to reach up to the Heavenly Realm, but is struck
down with a single blow as a reward for our impudence.

All that was is suddenly different.

The power of God creates diversity in destruction.

Each piece of the Tower remains intact and each is still required in order to complete the whole.

Humankind struggles with the task of keeping the pieces together and available.

We hasten to gather the pieces as they tumble down and are astonished by the diversity of shape
and form.

But all has been created **from** the One **by** the One.

Our task now is to seek out the Unity in the Diversity.

House of Illusion

The seventh group of paths within the Tree of Life

Emanating from the seventh sephira Netzach נצח they are as follows:

פ The Star צ The Moon and ק The Sun

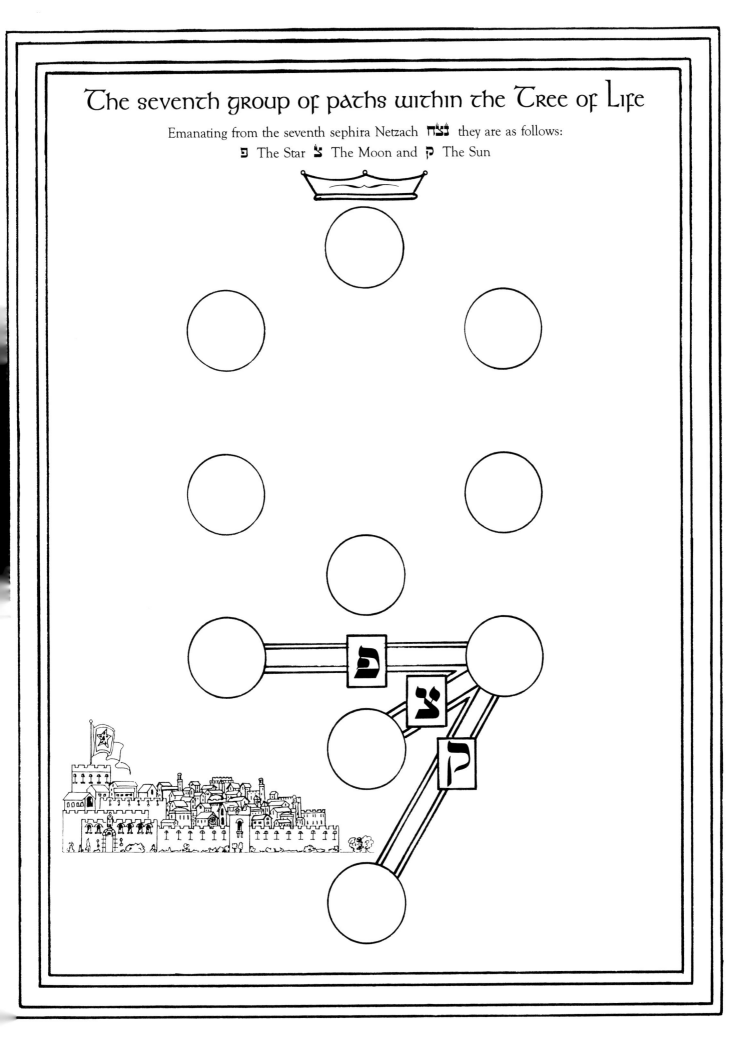

The Star   הכוכב

Path Twenty-seven   Peh   פ   פאה   נתיב העשרים ושביעית

Dweller Between the Waters   תושב בן המים

God Saw that It was Good

המליך אות פ׳ בממשלה וקשר לו כתר
וצרפן זה בזה וצר בהם כוכב בעולם יום חמישי בשנה
ואזן שמעל בנפש זכר ונקבה

God made the letter Peh king over governance and bound a crown to it
and made them one. With them, God made Mercury in the Universe,
all Thursdays in the Year and the Left Ear of the soul:
the Male and the Female

The Sensing Awareness שכל המרגש (*Sekhel HaMargash*), so called because the ability to use our senses to perceive those things that were created beyond the Veil lies on this path.

Path Twenty-seven connects the Water part of the seventh sephira Netzach נצח (victory) with the Water part of the eighth sephira Hod הוד (splendor). Our activities on this Path are greatly affected by the cycles and rhythms of the planet Mars מאדים (*madiim*).

The Creator gives the evening star dominion over the heavens and the earth. The city of our sleeping aspirations rests in the gentle glow of the stars above; unaware of the benevolent watchfulness which surrounds it.

In the midst of the heavens shines a great Star. Surrounding it are numerous smaller stars, their rays interwoven and penetrating all of Creation. A soft radiance fills the scene unfolding before us, and for a brief moment our perceptions are filled with an understanding of the Will, the Dreams and the Soul of Nature and of all the Worlds.

The sleeping city below is safe; the power of the heavens protecting the unaware inhabitants. We travel ever onwards as though we are in a dream; lives from the past, the present and the future meld in our reveries.

Our Visions and Imaginings are calm as we recall God's promise to Abraham sung during the Havdalah ceremony marking the conclusion of the Sabbath.
"I will bless you greatly, and increase your children like the stars set in the heavens and the sand by the seashore." Genesis 22:17.

Dweller between Waters

The Moon ‎הירח

Path Twenty-eight   Tzadi ‎צ   ‎צדי   ‎נתיב העשרים ושמונה

Ruler of Entropy   ‎משל התהו

God Blessed Them

‎המליך אות צ׳ בלעיטה וקשר לו כתר
‎וצרפן זה בזה וצר בהם דלי בעולם ושבט בשנה
‎וקורקבן בנפש זכר ונקבה

God made the letter Tzadi king over the Breath and bound a crown to
it and combined them. With them, God made Aquarius in the Universe,
Shevet in the Year and a Gizzard in the soul:
the Male with the Female

The **Natural Awareness** ‎שכל המטבע (*Sekhel HaMatba*), so called because it contains the source of the Veil ‎פרכת (*parochet*) between the knowledge of our sense of self as an individual and as part of creation as a whole.

Path Twenty-eight is the connection between the Air part of the seventh sephira Netzach ‎נצח (victory) and the Water part of the ninth sephira Yesod ‎יסוד (foundation).

On the fourth day, God set the Sun and the Moon in the Heavens. An Angel created on the second day sees before him the Four Rivers out of Eden creating the oceans of the world. In the distance a lone tower reaches toward the elemental rhythms of the moon.

The Angel came to Four Rivers and called gently to the waters so that they might praise The Almighty. God filled the waters with the forces that created life. And God Blessed Them by shining the face of the Moon into the dull wetness and thus formed the ripples of time.

We cross the waters and ascend into the Fields of Eden. The tower looms before us.... We begin to sense that the Tower is that of Babel. We are mistaken. We enter and watch as the ceiling opens to reveal all that is beyond. As our vision becomes adjusted to the moonlit heavens we feel the wisps of moonlight as they caress us.

The Angel attempted to arouse our natural instincts but we did not understand. Only as we basked in the heavenly glow could we allow ourselves to listen to our own voices in the silent dark night.

We have learned how to listen to our own needs and aspirations. We have taken the first major step to our goal.

RULER OF ENTROPY

The Sun   הַשֶּׁמֶשׁ

Path Twenty-nine   Kuf   ק   קוּף   נְתִיב הָעֶשְׂרִים וְתִשְׁעָה

Fire of the World   אֵשׁ הָעוֹלָם

God said, behold I have Given You

הִמְלִיךְ אוֹת ק׳ בִּשְׂחוֹק וְקָשַׁר לוֹ כֶּתֶר
וְצֶרְפָן זֶה בָּזֶה וְצֶר בָּהֶם דָּגִים בָּעוֹלָם וַאֲדָר בַּשָּׁנָה
וּטְחֹל בַּנֶּפֶשׁ זָכָר וּנְקֵבָה

He made the letter Kuf king over Laughter and bound a crown
to it and combined them. With them, God made Pisces in the
Universe, Adar in the Year and the Spleen in the soul:
Male and Female.

The Coarse Awareness שֵׂכֶל הַמֻגְשָׁם (*Sekhel HaMugsham*), so called because it provides the raw heat חמה (*chamah*) and the earth אֲדָמָה (*adomah*) required for the growth of all physical things.

Path Twenty-nine connects the Earth part of the seventh sephira Netzach נצח (victory) with the Fire part of the tenth sephira Malkhut מלכות (kingdom). This path contains the zodiacal sign of Pisces דָּגִים (*dagim*) and it is here that the seeds preserved in winter prepare for the transformations and the rebirth of spring.

As the Great Conqueror Alexander approaches the cynic philosopher Diogenes, he inquired of him if there was anything with which he could oblige or provide him. "Get out of my sunshine" replied the cynic. Alexander was amazed at the utter independence of this man who chose to live in a barrel. "If I were not Alexander, I would wish to be Diogenes"

The Sun beats down with its energy in the midst of the confrontation between the king and the philosopher. The rays blind our eyes but awaken our feelings. As the warmth penetrates, it relaxes us. We see the futility of the Emperor's request.

Clearly without the powers emanating from the Sun, neither earth nor moon could exist. Diogenes exemplifies the connectivity among these three heavenly bodies.

The mystical flower which began in the waters of the moon unfolds in the daylight. We are brought to the understanding that our Garden created in the safety of Malkhut, is always with us.

We understand that all of nature is continually born and re-born out of the mysteries exemplifying the union of the great angelic powers.

FIRE OF THE WORLD

The eighth group of paths within the Tree of Life

Emanating from the eighth sefira Hod הוד they are as follows:

ר Judgement and ש The World

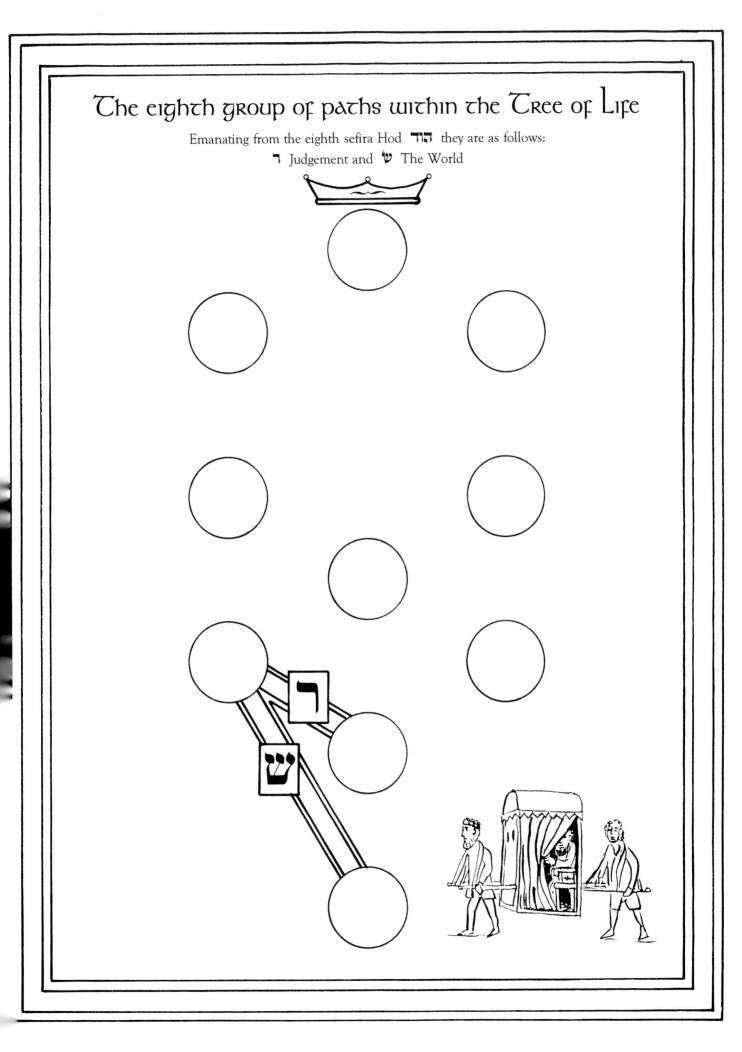

JUDGEMENT יום הדין

Path Thirty   **Resh** ר   רש   נתיב השלשים

SPIRIT OF THE PRIMAL FIRE   רוח אש הראשון

God saw that it was Good

המליך אות ר' בחכמה וקשר לו כתר
וצרפן זה בזה וצר בהם לבנה בעולם
יום ראשון בשנה ועין ימין בנפש זכר ונקבה

God made the letter Resh king over Peace and bound a crown to
it and combined them. With them, God made Saturn in the
Universe, Friday in the Year and the Left Nostril in the soul:
Male and Female.

The General Awareness שכל הכללי (*Sekhel HaKlali*), so called because it contains the means for the gathering of the knowledge of the Auphaniim wheels and the visions of Ezekiel which describe the forces that govern the stars and the constellations.

Path Thirty connects the Air part of the eighth sephira Hod הוד (splendor) with the Air part of the ninth sephira Yesod יסוד (foundation). When we travel this path we encounter all of the cosmological elements which have contact with the aspectual circle of the Sun.

The Archangels מלאכים גדולים במעלה (*malachim gdolim bema-aleh*) of the Four Quarters sound their trumpets alerting us to the ultimate re-birth and renewal of creation. The cities of the present, the past and the future rise in anticipation of the Messianic Promise.

The trumpets summon us from our natural complacency. The blaring sounds train us to respond to the impulse. We try to resist at first, but the vibrations leave us little choice. We react to the noise with an alarming regularity.

The tombs bring us future memory of what we must discard to continue on our journey. The head stones are the reminder that our lives create our own epitaph. We leave behind what binds us and travel past the city of our own thoughts.

The sun illuminates the Blue Mountain and beckons us onward. We reach beyond the antediluvian Titans whose domain does not extend beyond our perception.

We release our bonds with the physical world and are free from the necessity to control the mundane, we have been given the freedom to be aware of and be exposed to deeper forces.

SPIRIT of the PRIMAL FIRE

The World   הָעוֹלָם

Path Thirty-one	Shin	שׁ	נתיב השלשים ואחד שׁין

Your Kingdom is Everlasting   מלכותך מלכות כל עולמים

God made the Beasts of the Field

המליך אות שׁ' באש וקשר לו כתר
וצרפן זה בזה וצר בהם אש שמים וחום בשנה
וראש בנפשא זכר בשא״מ ונקבה בשמי״א

God made the letter Shin king over Fire and bound a crown to it
and combined them. With them, God made Heaven in the
Universe, Heat in the Year a Head in the soul: the Male with
ShAM, the Female with ShMA

The Ongoing Awareness שׂכל התמיד (*Sekhel HaTamid*), so called because it controls and directs the movements of the celestial bodies in the heavens, principally the Sun and the Moon.

Path Thirty-one connects the Earth part of the eighth sephira, Hod הוד (splendor) with the Water part of the tenth sephira Malkhut מלכות (kingdom). It contains all three Fire Signs: Aries, Leo and Sagittarius, and their qualities. On this path we are able to take direct control of the physical body through the powers of the mind.

The World of Creation is supported by one of the Titans נפילם (*nephilim*). We see the Sun, the Earth and the Moon surrounded by the zodiacal signs resting on his shoulders. He kneels on the ground burdened, but not overpowered by that which he bears. In the distance we see the city of the Giants, citadel of all that has been, facing out across a boundless ocean. A lone ship is on the horizon.

We gaze outwards from our garden. All of creation and all of eternity seems to impinge on our awareness. Our attention is distracted as this variety assails us. All is presented, the universe without and within. It seems as if the Titan would be overwhelmed.

He carries his heavy load with the knowledge that as we travel this path, we can learn the answer to his magical skill.

His ability to control the three zodiacal elements of Fire is personified by the Primal Yud י of the Divine Name in the world of Nobility.

We repeat this trial by Fire as we journey between our minds and our bodies. Each time we pass through we try to add another piece to our increasing sense of oneness with the World of Creation. If we succeed in our journey we can control our bodies with our minds and our minds with our bodies.

Your Kingdom Is Everlasting

The ninth and last grouping of the Tree of Life

Emanating from the ninth sephira Yesod **יסוד** and spilling into the World

ת is The Fool

The Fool　　　　　　　　　　　הַטִּפֵּשׁ

Path Thirty-two　　　　Tav　**ת**　　　תו　נתיב השלשים ושתים

Spirit of the Abyss　　**רוח השאול**

God saw all that He had Made

המליך אות ת' בחן וקשר לו כתר
וצרפן זה בזה וצר בהם צדיק בעולם ים
שבת ופה בנפש זכר ונקבה

God made the letter Tav king over Benevolence and bound a
crown to it and combined them. With them, God made Jupiter in
the Universe, The Sabbath in the Year and a Mouth in the soul:
Male and Female

The Cultivated Consciousness **שכל הנעבד** (*Sekhel HaNe-avad*), so called because God has tilled and prepared the ground where this path leads.

Path Thirty-two connects the Earth part of the ninth sephira Yesod **יסוד** (foundation), with the Fire part of the tenth sephira Malkhut **מלכות** (kingdom). This path is influenced by the aspectual circle of the planet Saturn **שבתאי** (*shavtai*).

The Fool wears the garb of accomplishment and shoulders the Tree of Life. He stumbles along oblivious to the dangers which surround him: the Lynx tries to slow his progress, the ravine yawns in his path, and the gaping maw of a huge crocodile awaits him in the river below.

The Fools calm demeanor is one of complacency rather than that of an inner peace, as we start our journey on the inner paths. Armed with perceived strengths, The Fool carries the Tree of Life with its thirty-two leaves accessible at all times. He doesn't use it as a staff to ease his journey. He does not understand that the Lynx is not part of the normal vicissitudes of life.

He wears the hat of a Master, but it is clear that he is unaccustomed to its weight. He plods ahead. He cannot yet lead. He takes the dangers in his stride, but does not identify them as harmful until they are overtaken.

We ask him. "What is it that you carry?" After a long while a voice answers us. "Do you not see that the tree needs to be planted?" "But we have just begun our journey. If we leave it here beyond the abyss we seek, we will never have access to it again."

The voice responded: "Fear no evil, for You are with Me; the staff and rod will comfort you."

Spirit of the Abyss

Glossary of Selected Terms

Aggadah
Aramaic: To tell. All non-legal material in the Talmud and Midrash, including astronomy, astrology, fables, folklore legends, medicine, proverbs and so on.

Amoraiim
Spokesmen. Those masters and teachers whose dissertations, known as the *Gemara* were written between 200 and about 500 C.E.

Apocrypha
The collections of anonymous ethical and historical works from the Second Temple period, not included in the Biblical canon because of their doubtful origin. The books of Maccabees and Judith are good examples of what the Rabbis considered worthy but extraneous writings.

Avot
The Mishnaic teachers of the third century B.C.E. who laid the foundations of Jewish legal interpretation. Also known as *Tannaiim*.

Baqqa
A Sufi term for perpetuity or the eternal.

Bava
Gate. When the Talmudic canon of civil law was divided into three parts, each was called a 'Gate'.

Chilleh
Turkish: A retreat. In the Mevlevi (whirling) order of dervishes the *chilleh* was for one thousand and one days.

Connectivity
The expression used to describe the idea of mutual relevance.

Fana
The Sufi term for annihilation in the context of passing from the manifest to the unmanifest, from the relative to the absolute.

Fikhr
Arabic: Reflection or meditation on some religious subject. This is performed by entering into a specific sequence of ideas or visualizations. See also *Zhikr*.

Gaon
The title bestowed on the heads of the Babylonian academy from the third to tenth centuries C.E.

Gemara
A vast discursive commentary on the Mishnah. Together with the Mishnah comprises the Talmud.

Gematria
From the Greek, *Geometria*. A form of cryptography in which words derive their meaning from the sum of the numbers contained in the Hebrew letters.

Hafiz
Protector of the Koran. One who knows the entire Koran by memory.

Haqq
In Sufism, the divine truth.

Haqqiya
Truth as divinity.

Haqua-iq
Hidden truths and qualities made possible by acts of annihilation (*fana*).

Halakha
The way to walk. The word used when referring to Jewish law in general.

Hasid	In Mishnaic times (3rd century B.C.E) the term was used to denote groups of militant anti-Roman Pharisees. In the eighteenth century the term was used to refer to the followers of R. Israel ben Eliezer, known as the Baal Shem Tov.
Itlak	The Sufi term for liberation in the sense of harmonizing or blending.
Kalb salim	A sound heart; is said to be the condition of direct vision experienced by Sufi masters.
Kavvanah	To give direction or turn toward. A directing of the attention towards the Creator in prayer or the performance of a commandment.
Khilafa	In the Sufi tradition, succession (to vicarship) achieved by a process of self annihilation.
Koran	The sacred book of Islam, containing the collected revelations of the Prophet, Mohammed.
Machzor	The Jewish prayer book containing the liturgy for the three Pilgrimage Festivals and the High Holy Days.
Madjhoub	One who is brought to a state of ecstasy by divine attraction without the need for conscious effort.
Magic	The various arts by which man has attempted to influence events.
Massekhet	Web. A section in, or book of traditional texts such as the Mishnah, Talmud or Tosephta.
Megillah	Rolled scroll. The five books of the Torah are Megillot, together with the Song of Songs, Ruth, Ecclesiastes, Lamentations and Esther.
Midrash	*Hebrew:* That which is sought. The literature and method of rabbinical literature that derives concealed meaning from traditional texts.
Mishnah	Study by repetition. The name given to the classical Six Orders of Halakhic material organized by Judah the Prince in about 200 C.E. Together with the Gemara, known as the Talmud.
Murid	*Arabic:* term applied to a novice during the period of preparation for entry into a Dervish order.
Nazir, Nazirite	The name or title which in biblical times was given to an individual who had taken a vow to abstain from ingesting grapes or grape products. A Nazirite also refrained from cutting the hair as a gesture of piety.
Notarikon	*Greek:* Shorthand writer. The name of a method of interpreting words and phrases in the Biblical canon which involves reading them as acronyms or as groups of smaller words.
Polarity	The intrinsic alignment of a force. The bioenergetic orientation of living things or the magnetic field of a planet or star, for example.

Rabban	Master. An honorary title of the head of the Sanhedrin.
Rabbi, R.	*Hebrew:* Teacher or Master. The title Rabbi can be used by Jewish teachers, leaders and judges.
Rebbe	*Yiddish:* The leader of a Hasidic community.
Salaat	Islamic ritual prayer or divine service, the highest goal of which is absorption into the Deity.
Sanhedrin	The highest court of Ancient Israel. Until 70 C.E. the Sanhedrin met in the Temple in Jerusalem, later in Yavneh, and eventually in Tiberius where it remained until 425 C.E. when its meeting was outlawed by the Romans. The Sanhedrin consisted of seventy members plus a *Nasi* (president or prince), for a total of seventy-one. When meeting together, it is said, the presence of God is invoked bringing the total to seventy-two.
Sema	In Sufi practice, a ceremony built around music. The celebrants participate by singing, chanting, recitation or the playing of musical instruments. Often these ceremonies include the performance of ritual movements or dances which are said to heighten the ecstatic experience.
Semazen	*Turkish:* A whirler in the turning dance of the Mevlevi order of Dervishes.
Sikkeh	*Turkish:* The tall felt hat often worn by Dervishes.
Siddur	The book containing the liturgy necessary for daily and Sabbath services.
Structure	That element of our experience that allows us to perceive the organic nature of wholeness.
Sufi, Sufism	The mystical tradition usually associated with Islam. The fundamental tenet of all branches of Sufism teaches that God has written each individual's truth upon the heart. If our hearts are cleansed from all personal selfhood, and trust is put in the heart, then we are able to recognize reality and God.
Takkanah	A change made in Jewish law by proclamation and not proven from Torah text.
Tanach	Torah (the Five Books of Moses), *Nevi'im* (Prophets) and *Ketuviim* (Writings). Hebrew name for the Bible. It is a acronym from the initial letters of the three major sections.
Tariqa	*Arabic:* The Way; the path of the dervish.
Tannaim	The name generally used for the scholars whose opinions constitute the text of the Mishnah.
Tassawuf	*Arabic:* The act of devoting oneself to the mystic life.
Torah	*Hebrew:* Teaching. One of the names given to the Pentateuch, the Five books of Moses.
Tzaddik	Righteous One or pious individual. Since the eighteenth century the term *Tzaddik* has occasionally been used as a title in Hasidic communities.

Will	The affirmative content in our experience. The ultimate source of the "how and why" of the universe.
Yeshiva	*Hebrew*: Sitting. The word for a traditional Talmudic academy.
Zhikr	*Arabic*: The remembrance of God. In Sufi and Dervish orders the repetition of one or more of the names of God are commonly used as the Zhikr. Allah, Allah, Allah or Hu, Hu, Hu are typical examples.

Bibliography of Works in English

Abdullah Yusuf Ali	*The Holy Koran*	New Delhi	1993
Abelson, J.	*The Immanence of God in Rabbinical Literature*	London	1912
Abelson, J.	*Jewish Mysticism*	London	1913
Anderson, Margaret	*The Fiery Fountains*	New York	1969
Arasteh, Reza	*Rumi, the Persian, the Sufi*	Tucson	1972
Arberry, A. J.	*Sufism*	London	1950
Arnold, Edwin	*Pearls of Faith*	London	1886
Bancroft, Ann	*Twentieth Century Mystics and Sages*	Chicago	1976
Bar-Lev, R. Yechiel	*Yedid Nefesh*	Petach Tikva	1988
Bennett, John G.	*Witness*	London	1962
Bennett, John G.	*Intimations*	London	1975
Bennett, John G.	*The Masters of Wisdom*	London	1976
Berg, Phillip S.	*An Entrance to the Tree of Life*	Jerusalem	1977
Bension, Ariel	*The Zohar in Moslem and Christian Spain*	London	1932
Birge, John K.	*The Bekhtashi Order of Dervishes*	London	1965
Brown, John P.	*The Darvishes (or Oriental Spiritualism)*	London	1968
Burckhardt, Titus	*The Darvishes*	Lahore	1959
Burke, Omar M.	*Among the Dervishes*	New York	1975
Butler, Bill	*The Definitive Tarot*	London	1975
Collins, Rodney	*The Theory of Celestial Influence*	New York	1974
Connolly, Eileen	*Tarot: The Handbook for the Journeyman*	Van Nuys	1987
Crowley, Aleister.	*777 Anthology*	York Beach	1973
Doreal, M.	*Sepher Yetzirah*, trans: and analysis	Denver	1941
Eisen, William	*The Cabalah of Astrology*	Marina del Rey	1986
Fakhry, M.	*A History of Islamic Philosophy*	New York	1970
Feldenkrais, Moshe	*Awareness through Movement*	New York	1972
Franck, A.	*The Kabbalah*	New York	1926
Frankel / Teutsch	*The Encyclopedia of Jewish Symbols*	Northvale	1992
Franklin, Stephen	*Origins of the Tarot Deck*	Jefferson	1988
Friedlander, Ira	*The Whirling Dervishes*	New York	1975
Friedman, Irving	*Book of Creation*, trans. and commentary	New York	n.p.
Gaster, M.	*The Maaseh Book*, trans.	Philadelphia	1934
Gray, William G.	*The Sangreal Tarot*	York Beach	1988
Hasbrouck, Muriel	*Tarot and Astrology*	Wellingborough	1986
Hourani, G.	*Essays on Islamic Philosophy*	Albany	1975
Iqbal, Afzal	*Life and Work of Rumi*	Lahore	1956
Jacobs, Louis	*The Palm Tree of Deborah*, trans.	London	1960
Kalish, Isidor	*A Book on Creation*, trans.	New York	1877

Kaplan, Aryeh	The Book of Creation	York Beach	1993
Kaplan, Aryeh	The Bahir	York Beach	1989
Kaplan, Aryeh	Torah (The Living) trans.	New York	1981
MacGregor Mathers, S. L.	The Key of Solomon, trans.	York Beach	1989
Mordel, Phineas	Sefer Yetzirah. trans.	Philadelphia	1894
Mordel, Phineas	The Origin of Letters and Numerals (reprint)	York Beach	1975
Myer, Isaak	Quabbalah, trans. writings of Ibn Gavirol	Philadelphia	1888
Nasr, Seyyed H.	Sufi Essays	London	1972
Nasr, Seyyed H.	Islamic Cosmological Doctrines	London	1978
Nasr, Seyyed H.	Al-Biruni: An Annotated Biography	Tehran	1973
Nicholson, R. A.	The Sufi Orders of Islam	London	1962
Odeberg, Hugo	Hebrew Book of Enoch, trans.	London	1926
Peach, Edward (Ophiel)	The Art and Practice of Caballa Magic	New York	1981
Pollack, Rachel	Tarot: The Open Labyrinth	Wellingborough	1986
Raskin, Saul	Kabbalah in Word and Image	New York	1952
Regardie, Israel	A Garden of Pomegranates, trans.	St Paul	1970
Rizvi, S. A.	History of Sufism in India	Delhi	1983
Sayid Sheikh, M	Studies in Muslim Philosophy	Lahore	1962
Schimmel, Anne-Marie	Mystical Dimensions of Islam	Carolina	1975
Scholem, Gershom G.	On the Kabbalah and Its Symbolism	New York	1970
Scholem, Gershom G.	Major Trends in Jewish Mysticism	New York	1961
Schuon, Frithjof	Dimensions of Islam, trans.	London	1969
Schuon, Frithjof	Understanding Islam	London	1963
Shah, Idries	The Sufis	New york	1964
Shah, Idries	The Way of the Sufi	London	1968
Shushud, Hasan	Masters of Wisdom of Central Asia	London	1983
Singh, Kirpal	Naam or Word	Delhi	1972
Spain, Gary	Table Zero	Unpublished	
Stenring, Knut	The Book of Formation, trans.	London	1923
Subhan, J. A.	Sufism, Its Saints and Shrines	New York	1970
Sumohadiwidjojo, M.	Subud	Gjovic	1959
Talmud	Various editions and translations		
Trachtenberg, Joshua	Jewish Magic and Superstition	New York	1939
Trimingham, J.Spencer	The Sufi Orders in Islam	London	1971
Underhill, Evelyn	Mysticism	Cambridge	1928
Valiudin, Dr. Mir	Contemplative Disciplines in Sufism	London	1980
Waite, Arthur E.	The Holy Kabbalah	London	1929
Waite, Arthur E.	Pictorial Key to the Tarot	New York	1929
Walzer, R.	Greek into Arabic	Oxford	1962
Wang, Robert	Tarot Psychology	Sauerlauch	1988
Wanless, James	Voyager Tarot	Carmel	1989
Webb, James	The Harmonious Circle	New York	1980

Westcott, William	*Sepher Yetzirah, The Book of Formation*	York Beach	1975
Williams-Heller, Ann.	*Kabbalah*	London	1990
Wolfson, H.A.	*The Amphibolous Terms in Aristotle Arabic Philosophy and Maimonides*	Harvard	1938
Work of the Chariot (pseudonym)	*Book of Formation*, trans.	Los Angeles	1970
Zelazny, Roger	*Trumps of Doom*	New York	1986
Ziegler, G.	*Tarot: Mirror of the Soul*	York Beach	1988
Zohar	Various editions and translations		

Bibliography of Hebrew and Arabic Sources

Manuscripts and early printed material. Mostly the British Museum (London), Bibliotheque National (Paris), Israel Museum (Jerusalem), Tel Aviv University, Vatican Library (Rome), Jewish Theological Seminary (Cincinatti), Hebrew Union College (New York), Oxford University, Cambridge University, The Israel Museum (Jerusalem) and many others.

10th century	Oxford, Ms. Oppenheim 1010.
10th century	Paris, Ms. 1048:2.
10th century	Berlin, Ms. Or 243:4.
10th century	Vatican, Ms. 299, ff. 66a-71b.
11th century	Geniza Fragment, Taylor Shechter 32.5
11th century	Geniza Fragment, Cambridge-Westminster, Talmud 23-25.
13th century	Paris, Ms. 770:1.
13th century	Oxford, Ms. 1598:3.
13th century	Oxford, Ms. 1531, ff. 1b-12a.
14th century	British Museum, Ms Gaster 415, ff. 29a-32a.
14th century	HUC Cincinatti, Ms. 523.
14th century	Paris, Ms. 802, ff. 57b-59b.
14th century	Parma, Ms. 1390, ff. 36b-38b.
14th century	British Museum, Ms. 737, ff. 379b-387a.
14th century	British Museum, Ms. 754, ff. 212a-216a.
15th century	Paris, Ms. 770, ff. 41a-45a.
16th century	Cambridge, Ms. Add 647, ff. 7b-9b.
16th century	Oxford, Ms. 2455, ff. 3a-8b.
16th century	Vatican, Ms. 441, ff. 118a-122a.
16th century	Cambridge, Ms. Add 10862.
16th century	British Museum, Ms. Sl 1307.
17th century	Oxford, Ms. Kings 288.
17th century	Oxford, Ms. Harleian 3981.
17th century	Landsdowne, Ms. 1202.
17th century	Landsdowne, Ms. 1203.

Moses Cordovero	פרדס רמונים	Cracow	1592
Elijah de Vilas	ס׳ ראשית הכמה	Venice	1593
Joseph Gikatila	גנת אגוז	Hanau	1614
Joseph Gikatalia	שערי אורת	Offenbach	1715
Moses Luzzatto	קל״ם פתחי הכמה	Koretz	1785
Simeon ibn Labi	כתם פז	Lvorno	1795
Adolf Jellinek	גנזי הכמת הקבלה	Leipzig	1853
Hayim Vital	ס׳ עץ חיים	Warsaw	1891
Avraham Azulai	אור החמה	Przemysl	1896
Israel Saruk	למדי אצילות	Muncacs 1897	
Jekutiel Kamelhar	חסידים הראשונים	Weitzen	1917
Avraham Kook	אורת	Jerusalem	1921

Note: there is some availability to this material through photostatic and digitized images.

Bibliography of Works in Other Languages

French

Alleau, R.	*Aspects de l'Achemie Traditionelle*	Paris	1953
Carra de Vaux	*Les Penseurs de l'Islam*	Paris	1926
Cassanova, P.	*Alphabets Magiques Arabes*	Paris	1922
Comptesse Calomira de Cimarra	*Sepher Yetzirah*	Paris	1913
Gilson, E.	*L'Esprit de la Philosophie Medievale*	Paris	1932
Jean Doresse	*Les Livres Secrets des Gnostiques d'Egypte*	Paris	1958
Jean Rene Legrand	*Meditations Cabbalistiques*	Paris	1955
Karppe	*Etude sur les Origines du Zohar*	Paris	1901
Meyer Lambert	*Commentaire sur le Sepher Yetzirah*	Paris	1891
Schuon, F.	*Comprendre l'Islam*	Paris	1976

German

Kaufmann, D.	*Studien zur Salomon ibn Gabirol*	Budapest	1899
Lazarus Goldschmidt	*Das Buch der Schopfung (Sepher Jesirah)*	Frankfort	1894
Yohann von Meyer	*Das Buch Yezirah*	Leipzig	1830
Gershom Sholem	*Bibliographica Kabbalistica*	Leipzig	1927

Latin

Athanasius Kirscher	*Werke Oedipus Aegyptus 2:1*	Rome	1653
Johannes Pistorius	*Artis Cabalisticae hoc est Reconditae Theoloiae Philosophiae Scriporum.*	Basille	1587
Gulelmus Postellus	*Abrahami Patriarchae Liber Jezirah sive Formationis Mundi...*	Paris	1552
Joanne Rittangelio	*Liber Jezirah, qui Abrahamos Patriarchae Adscribitur unacum Commentario Rabi Abraham F.D.*	Amsterdam	1642

Appendix One

A table of Correspondence between the letters of the Hebrew alphabet, the Tarot Trumps the Paths of the Tree of Life and their Titles

א	The Magician	path 11 The Polished Awareness	Magus of Power
ב	The High Priestess	path 12 The Bright Awareness	Priestess of the Star
ג	The Empress	path 13 The Directing Awareness	Daughter of the Titans
ד	The Emperor	path 14 The Illuminated Awareness	Lord of the Dawn
ה	The High Priest	path 15 The Supporting Awareness	Lord of Eternity
ו	The Lovers	path 16 The Enduring Awareness	Children of the Voice
ז	The Chariot	path 17 The Sensory Awareness	The Triumph of Light
ח	Strength	path 18 The Awareness of Influx	Child of the Spinning Sword
ט	The Hermit	path 19 The Spiritual Awareness	Promise of the Eternal
י	Wheel of Fortune	path 20 The Awareness of Will	Master of Force
כ	Justice	path 21 The Desired Awareness	Daughter of Truth
ל	The Hanged Man	path 22 The Faithful Awareness	Spirit of the Endless Waters
מ	Death	path 23 The Sustaining Awareness	The Great Transformer
נ	Temperance	path 24 The Imagining Awareness	Spirit of Life
ס	The Devil	path 25 The Experimenting Awareness	Father of Lies
ע	The Tower	path 26 The Renewing Awareness	House of Illusion
פ	The Star	path 27 The Sensing Awareness	Dweller Between the Waters
צ	The Moon	path 28 The Natural Awareness	Ruler of Entropy
ק	The Sun	path 29 The Course Awareness	Fire of the World
ר	Judgement	path 30 The General Awareness	Spirit of the Primal Fire
ש	The World	path 31 The Ongoing Awareness	Your Kingdom Is Everlasting
ת	The Fool	path 32 The Cultivated Awareness	Spirit of the Abyss

Appendix Two

Foreign language titles of Tarot Trumps

Hebrew	French	German	Italian
המכשׁף	Le Bateleur	Der Magier	Il Mago
כהנת הגדולה	Junon	Die Hohepriesterin	La Papessa
הקיסרית	L'Imperatrice	Die Herrscherin	L'Imperatrice
הקיסר	L'Empereur	Der Herrscher	L'Imperatore
הכהן הגדול	Jupiter	Der Hohepriester	Il Papa
האהבים	L'Amoreux	Die Liebenden	L'Amore
המרכבה	Le Chariot	Der Triumphwagen	Il Carro
העצמה	La Justice	Gerichtigkeit	La Giustizia
הנזיר	L'Ermite	Der Eremit	Il Gobbo
גלגל המזל	La Roue de Fortune	Das Glucksrad	La Fortuna
שׁופטות	La Force	Die Kraft	La Forza
התלוי	Le Pendu	Der Aufgehangte	Il Penduto
המות	La Mort	Der Tod	Il Morte
מתינמות	La Temperance	Der Ausgleich	La Temperanza
יצר הרע	Le Diable	Der Teufel	Il Diavolo
המגדל	La Tour	Der Turm	La Torre
הכוכב	L'Etoile	Der Stern	La Stella
הירח	La Lune	Der Mond	La Luna
השׁמשׁ	Le Soleil	Die Sonne	Il Sole
יום הדין	Le Jugemont	Das Gericht	Il Giudizio
העולם	Le Monde	Die Welt	Il Mondo
הטפשׁ	Le Mat	Der Narr	Il Matto

Appendix Three

Correspondences between the Sephirot of the Tree of Life and Tarot

כתר	Keter	Crown	1st Path	The Mystical	Four Aces
חכמה	Hokhmah	Wisdom	2nd Path	The Radiant	Four Twos
בינה	Binah	Understanding	3rd Path	The Sanctified	Four Threes
חסד	Hesed	Grace	4th Path	The Settled	Four Fours
גברה	Gevurah	Strength	5th Path	The Rooted	Four Fives
תפארת	Tiferet	Beauty	6th Path	The Transcendant	Four Sixes
נצח	Netzach	Eternity	7th Path	The Concealed	Four Sevens
הוד	Hod	Grandeur	8rh Path	The Complete	Four Eights
יסוד	Yesod	Foundation	9th Path	The Pure	Four Nines
מלכות	Malkhut	Kingdom	10th Path	The Gleaming	Four Tens

Appendix Four

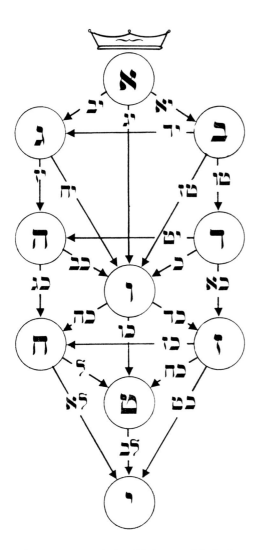

The Letters of the Hebrew Alphabet

Used as Numbers. In this method the 10 Sefirot are considered paths within the structure of the Tree of Life. Thus, the total number of paths is thirty-two. This scheme was and still is much favored by students of Gematria and manufacturers of Talismans and Amulets (קמעות).

The Letters of the Hebrew Alphabet

Represented as names of the Sephirot (paths 1–10), and as symbols of the 22 connectivities paths of the Tree of Life (paths 11–32). The pattern followed by the author in this work.

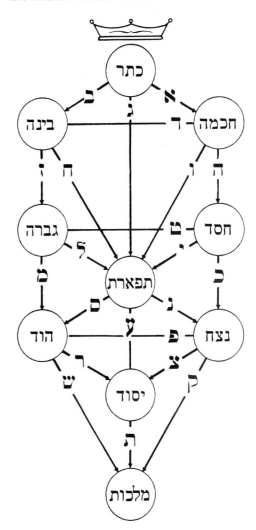

Appendix Five

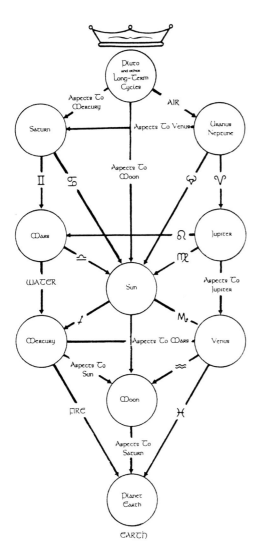

The Paths of the Tree of Life

With their Astrological correspondences. Although the Astrology of the Kabbalah is not the subject of this work it is interesting to note that the early Kabbalists were much influenced by the cosmological doctrines of their Sufi contempories, in particular the writings of Ibn Sina (Avicenna) and al-Biruni.

The paths of the Tree of Life

The relationship between the Arcana of the Tarot, the Sefirot, and the Paths of the Tree of Life.

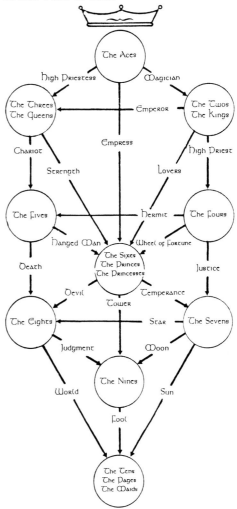

Appendix Six

The Tree of Life

The Sephirot connected in the manner of a Lightning Strike.

The Sefirot of the Tree of Life

Transliteration of the Hebrew name.
Translation of the Hebrew name.
The author's suggested correspondance with contemporary word usage.

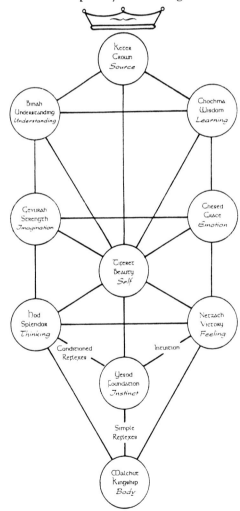

Appendix Seven

Permutations of the Hebrew Alphabet

Number of letters	Number of permutations
1	1
2	2
3	6
4	24
5	120
6	720
7	5,040
8	40,320
9	362,880
10	3,628,800
11	39,916,800
12	479,001,600
13	6,227,020,800
14	87,178,291,200
15	1,307,674,368,000
16	20,922,789,888,000
17	355,687,428,096,000
18	6,402,373,705,728,000
19	121,645,100,408,832,000
20	2,432,902,008,176,640,000
21	51,090,942,171,709,440,000
22	1,124,000,727,777,607,680,000

Afterword

As a young artist setting out on the road to conquer the world, I planned first of all to paint the entire biblical Canon.

Some forty years later I am still trying to paint myself out of Genesis!

It is my hope that this work will provide the readers with a key with which to explore and express their own inspiration while enjoying the wonderful realms of religious, mystical, and philosophical literature.

M.J.
Venice, California

About the Artist/Author

Michael Jacobs is an artist living in Venice, California. His artistic style is influenced by his studies of Persian miniature painting, Buddhist art, Koranic calligraphy and Hebrew calligraphy. Jacobs continues to pursue work in Fourth Way Studies, cosmology, Kabbalah, and the visual arts. Throughout a lifetime of travel, Michael Jacobs has endeavored to perpetuate and foster knowledge and understanding. *Ten and Twenty-Two* is his first book.

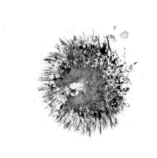